Finding me —and Them

Stories of Assimilation

MICHAEL P. AMRAM

WESTBOW
PRESS®
A DIVISION OF THOMAS NELSON
& ZONDERVAN

WestBow Press books may be ordered through booksellers or by contacting:

WestBow Press
A Division of Thomas Nelson & Zondervan
1663 Liberty Drive
Bloomington, IN 47403
www.westbowpress.com
1 (866) 928-1240

ISBN: 978-1-5127-8199-1 (sc)
ISBN: 978-1-5127-8198-4 (hc)
ISBN: 978-1-5127-8200-4 (e)

Library of Congress Control Number: 2017905050

Print information available on the last page.

WestBow Press rev. date: 04/13/2017

Foreword

*L*ooking at these stories as an expert witness, they are a recipe for me. They're who I've become. I appreciate and understand things in life because of what I've done, because of where I've been. They are greater concepts homogenized from wonderful or painful experiences. Concepts like fortitude, faith and spirituality, and compromise for love and maturity wait in these stories. They wait for the random reader to thumb to a page and find if there's any universality to my life or if it's so entirely unique the reader wants to thumb again. Is it not the goal of most disabled children to fit in, to be accepted and not always be the odd man? Depending on where one thumbs, they find it is a universal need, in the beginning anyway, to fit in somewhere, to not constantly be rejected, to sometimes be better than the odd man.

Many of these stories have borne a life of their own. They have hindsight. Many have ancient souls. This prose has had many incarnations and, in a few cases, enjoyed an afterlife. The first story in this book was written sometime in the early 1990s. Some have grown with me. I wrote them as I saw life seeing me at the time. I rewrote them with the ways I'd changed in my mind. I exercised demons in my salad days, I channeled my aggression, I tried to become the least odd man out that I could. Those were the facts, they were how I told myself prosaically. I show what actually happened. I write fiction of what might be, what I might like to be if things had turned out differently.

Contents

Foreword...v

1. Being the Greatest..1
2. My Day of Reckoning...6
3. A Lesson from the Shema..11
4. A Gentler Place 18
5. The Cheeky Lad 23
6. Exercising Demons 28
7. Ramifications of Schadenfreude.................................... 39
8. The Divining Weeks... 83
9. The Burial Plot 92
10. The Genuine Article 100

Afterword.. 129
About the Author 131

To Kathy

Being the Greatest

*T*he sun was setting when we reached our cabin. I heard the plaintive cry of a loon and felt July winds pressing my head softly. I swung my metal-based canes out of our maroon station wagon. Late afternoon water-skiers did their last run for the day. I rose from the car and heard an outboard motor idling. I imagined a skier reclined in the water, holding his ski tips parallel and out of the water, as if God had given him skis for feet. "Tension. . .hit it!"echoed through my new summer world, and that motor boat roared to full speed.

My training camp

When I was six years old, my father took me on long walks at our summer cabin in Northern Minnesota. It was the summer of 1971 and I was rehabilitating after a traumatic head injury that happened early in January that year. In March, a therapist started coming to the house. She worked with me until I could stand. My father took over then. We walked in a large, heated office garage near our home in the cities. I had very wide-based metal canes.

"Concentrate," he said, over and over–until I did.

It became a mantra, a voice that I could say in my head. My eyes focused on circles of salt on the floor. My father counted steps. In the quiet of the garage I heard the "click" of the silver counter he held tightly. But if I listened closely, almost in tandem, I heard a clod of snow fall from a bumper.

Our cabin was special to me, a retreat from the pressures of the cities. It fit conveniently between Bay and Tame Fish lakes. I was a fan of Muhammad Ali and imagined the cabin was a training camp like his. My father and I always watched his fights together. Ali danced in the ring and brought boxing to an art. I was drawn to his "float like a butterfly and sting like a bee" technique. I loved watching him effortlessly dispensing a salvo of jabs and uppercuts until his opponent was sufficiently mesmerized by his dance. His adversaries dropped to the canvas mechanically, every time, proving Ali's claims to be "the greatest" were not hyperbole.

φ

Bay Lake was large with distant bays. It was not deep and better for skiing than fishing. I watched as my dad, sister or mom water skied from our speed boat. Everything, from carrying the ski equipment across a road at the end of our driveway to locking up the boat, was a father and daughter activity. I was only able to watch. I sat in the boat as an observer, or was simply too tired (from our morning walk) or too timid to cross the road. I waited in one of the big Adirondack chairs in back of our cabin. My sister returned, and we fished from the dock as the sun set on the deeper and smaller lake.

Skiing on Bay Lake

Moored to our dock on Tame Fish lake was a row boat powered by a small outboard motor. The first summer after the accident all I was able to do was to lie on it. I was pulled on a blue hollow "zip" sled. Through the spray in my face, I saw my father sinking as the bow rose high. The sled had a rope handle. A rung of wood was between two braids of rope extending from the sled. It was modified it with a higher handle. The summer of 1971 it just dangled in front of me, coaching me to stand on the sled.

φ

The smell of pines and the sounds of woodpeckers toiling in desolate woods were conducive to learning to walk. They created an atmosphere that nurtured independence. The clean air, sounds of nature and skiers gave me an indomitable feeling. Gems of sun peeked through the trees as we walked. They shimmered off the water, gently assessing my progress as my father and I made our way down a winding, pot-holed country road. The general store was a half-mile from our cabin. It was a good non-negotiable distance. It became a benchmark on County Road 10. The store was always filled with gossip that told Bay Lake Township's story. Minnows were scooped in nets from tanks into metal buckets topped with holes. Night crawlers were sold in small, brown boxes.

The spots indicating that we were getting warmer became apparent to me. Eventually I knew the cabins and the clusters of mailboxes where resorts hid along the road. They triggered my anticipation. By trial and error, I learned to quell that subconscious advance in my pace that might cause me to fall. If I fell, the continuous click of the counter being wound back to zero was all I heard. Step one was taken–again–to the next reward. My goal was 400 steps without a fall. I walked my way to hotel weekends or dinners at fancy restaurants. My canes had lime green, vinyl, sand-filled weights wrapped at the base. Each month the weight decreased. Usually on our walk there was a distant clank of an old pickup truck that agitated the breeze. The dull whir of speedboat motors, followed by the halcyon cry of the water skier, made me think of the wakes they cut. I kicked up dust in mimicry.

The half mile was ten if it was a foot. I was tired. My legs ached. They quivered at the store's screen door. My father, never nurturing dependence, left the door for me to open. I slowly entered and was blind until my eyes adjusted to the dimmer light. The open tanks were in rows opposite the counter. Minnows darted about, seeming to know their fate. Adjacent to the bait and tackle section sprawled candy, ice cream bars and various grocery items as far as a six year old could see. The sweet smells of bubble gum and ice cream cones tempted me. I felt I had earned something by walking to the store. I humbly tried to charm myself a treat.

"You walked all this way? What can I get you honey?"

A middle-age woman with coarse, rusty hair and the toughened skin of an iron- ranger was behind the counter. I blinked my blue eyes, shuffled my canes like Ali, and usually emerged from that store with a treat. Those were the moments I felt I was "the greatest."

My Day of Reckoning

*S*cott pushed me and I tumbled back to earth. He stood, smug with his agility, near the top of the hill laughing at me.

"Give it up boy, you can't climb anything."

Sometimes the darker color of my skin filtered in as a convenient compliment to the disability taunts. Clever variations of the word Negro slid from the blissfully ignorant tongues of intolerance. Seven boys played King of the Hill in a corner of the schoolyard. The hill amounted to a pile of dirt about seven feet high, but it stood to divide and be conquered. I never won, never conquered anything and division had begun the day I stepped in that school.

In September of 1973, I re-entered Central Elementary after a two-season sabbatical in which I went to Michael Dowling School in Minneapolis. My kindergarten year at Central had started in the fall of 1970 and a closed head injury that winter required that I change my school of lower education. (In 1971, the school–established in 1920 and named for frostbitten amputee and Speaker of the Minnesota House of Representatives Michael Dowling–existed on the Mississippi River's west bank as a school for the disabled.)

The hill was small, but it was big to fourth graders. It was big to me, and I foolishly thought–I dreamed–of knocking Scott or Chris off its summit. I got burned routinely by bullies on my re-entry the first year back to Central. They were all new, sneering, jeering faces because the friends I'd walked to kindergarten with before I acquired–or required–crutches had progressed in the normal course to the fifth grade.

Routine recess sessions of alienation were coming to an end. Most of me was grateful. There was one small part, though, that did keep hope alive. A gut feeling that those bullies' day would come when the "crip" came out on top always accentuated my lunches. Those mid-day trips to stand in the line for hot lunch were ending soon. My wooden crutches slid on shiny green floors led by sloppy Joe scents burning my nose. It was early in June and the '73-'74 school year palpably drew to a close. The smell of paste blended with the meandering hum of a custodian's lawnmower coming through the parted windows. I felt the warmth of the sun, imagining it as a prelude to my summer away from a camp of hostility. In time, the sun shadowed the school's eaves, causing me to daydream to the rounds of the janitor's mowing machine until I realized that this was the last day to leave a mark on my painfully insecure classmates.

The bell rang and we were officially free from using our brains for the next three months. I slipped my arms into the canvas cuffs on my crutches that circled at my elbows. I bounded through the tiny coat room. We assembled just outside the classroom for a brief talk and I waited for some words from my teacher, my sole ally in school, which could give me an inkling of vindication over my classmates. He led us, like a pied piper of Central Elementary, and stopped at the door. He turned and gazed over us and his eyes seemed to spot me in back. He looked at his clipboard–around which his whistle hung–and said something that read me like a book.

"As a final event to our Olympics, we will have a slow bike race."

Events had been going on throughout the week, few of which I had any chance of honestly competing in, let alone winning. I felt a smile turn my face and I asked myself if it was terribly arrogant for me to think this had been designed for me–a race that I had virtually no chance of losing. Our gym teacher knew of the adult trike I rode to school sometimes. I happened to ride it that day.

Clusters of kids shouted as they moved toward the door. It was an angry mob moving to lynch a laughing classmate who brought up the rear. I would not be there for the lynching as gravity commanded them to move forward.

"Hey, what gives?" "He can't be in this race." "No crips allowed!"

The words hurt, but I smiled, knowing they'd soon eat them with dirt. I adopted myself as man of the hour and imagined I had a police escort to the big green doors. Mr. Goldman, our gym teacher, opened them and my eyes shot through the sunlight to my three wheels on the bike rack. I stabbed my crutch tips outside of the yellow hopscotch lines on the asphalt and cantered slowly to the rack. It was at my leisure now, the ball was in my court and I could, for this moment, afford to lose anything my handicap had taken away.

"You'll get yours; we'll put you in your place somehow!"

I fumbled with my keys, basking in my immunity to the schoolyard japes. I was fueled by my sense of eminence and the taste of imminent vengeance for the past year of psychological abuse. Next to me, on back wheels, was a long line of banana seats and ape-hanger handle bars. There, marinating in the hallowed dust of the schoolyard, stood the pride and joy of about fifty pre-pubescent boys. The bikes were the wheelie-popping testosterone boosters of boys not ready to be mindful of their tongues.

"Hey, that's not fair! He can't do this. He'll win for sure."

The lunch lady had one more meal to make. Its words were now being served for Scott to eat. I smiled broadly and savored every ounce of hostility the situation incited. Reprisal was a non-existent factor. Following the race, I would not have to see my adversaries for three months, at which time the matter would likely be forgotten.

Mr. Goldman arranged orange cones at either end of the ground, marking the starting point of the race.

"Disqualify him!"

"Hey, this is rigged. I'm not racing."

Some did forfeit, to my delight, although enough remained in the race to make victory sweet. I was the tortoise in this fable and I jockeyed my three-wheeler across the grounds to the line. Our wheels towed the line, keeping it fair that far. It was all sleek two-wheel sting-rays, baseball cards in spokes, tassels hanging off handle bars and me, inches above everyone with the breadth of my back wheels breaking dust that had often covered me.

"On your marks, get set …"

Bikes wobbled away from the line. Riders marshaled every ounce of balance, usually standing in the saddle. I did not move and let my competition get a head start. The forty or so "hares" rode in a jerky style, sitting down to peddle when gravity necessitated it. I taunted.

"Is that hard? Are you having fun? Who's king of the hill now?"

They looked back at me in fits of agility mixed with embarrassment and anger. At that point I had advanced inches beyond the line, remembering the loss of the fabled cocky hare. My competitors had done their best; they'd extrapolated all that they could from their youthful balance. Ahead of me, banana seats started to sway and one by one the schoolyard became a sea of fallen ape-hangers and the little rectangular license plates that belonged to the likes of Scott or Chris. Sometimes they made up derogatory names that slurred my ethnicity. When the crutch no longer filled their repertoire of derision, they might jibe on something as inbred as my curly black hair.

"I'll get you!"

I laughed while teachers cheered. They appeared to lead the few mates who were on the fence about how they should treat the kid with the crutches. I looked around at my fallen comrades and waited until the last one fell. I peddled across the finish line.

"As winner of the 1973 Central Elementary Olympics overall I award a white ribbon to Jeff Boyd."

Mr. Goldman stood with his clip board announcing winners of various events. I waited patiently, still the villain, the cheater that did not deserve to win.

"And, for today's final event, the white ribbon goes to Michael Amram."

"Boo, he cheated" or "But Mr. Goldman ..."

My opponents contested as though they had a leg to stand on, for it had been a slow bike race, and a ribbon had my name on it. I was the undisputed winner of 1974's slow bike race.

A Lesson from the Shema

I blinked and the black stripes on the rabbi's tallis (prayer shawl) grazed the whites of my eyes. I nodded off once or many times more during the service. I realized where I was, that we were still some place warm and friendly in the anonymity of the congregation. I was surrounded by more than eighty Reform Jews–surely more pious than myself. I asked myself what I was doing there, if I could sincerely say I was there for a purpose.

The uplifting words of the *Shema* always sounded good to me. This chant is said twice during the Sabbath service honoring Israel. It was helpful during my trying adolescence. The strength of the statement increased each time it was said. Each incantation I felt the bullies take another hit. The cantor led his congregation in the same way: sharply rising and falling, rising delicately and falling again. It was recited at the beginning of the service and then re-canted for edification. But the second time the congregation rose again and eventually sank back into their seats, sensing that the rabbi was wrapping up the service. I stood tall and proud for the Shema, with my chest out, occasionally mouthing the words. Mostly, though, I was stretching from the transcendent naps in which snippets of sermonizing sublimated my mind.

The cantor complemented the rabbi's efforts. The new ideas and weekly words of worship were posed by our rabbi, but the cantor really sold them through song, with the harsh intonation and dramatic enunciation Hebrew sometimes requires. After the Shema, I nodded off again to mumbles of the Kaddish in which the indistinguishable names of the dearly departed were read. The rabbi always called them out to his congregation with a tenderness that was hard to ignore. My sister and parents listened intently. It was usually during these weekly words of prayer that I had my naps. They were trite and young minds usually hunger for something new, something they can use today–not seventy years down the road. Some fifteen-year-olds can't appreciate anything that precedes their own gratification, especially in the course of a worship service. I had the Oneg Shabbat on my mind. This was the refreshment phase of the temple experience that consisted of flaky pastries, thick, gummy sweet cakes, cookies and powdered sugar rolls. They always inherited the smell of the temple. It was a stagnant, but strong, piercing smell that holds your nose the younger and more impressionable you are. Always, the taste was ethnic, exotically bland, tangy and sweet. The sweetness was not a gentile sweet; it was a subtle, sugary mélange that chose its buds cautiously as it rested on the tongue while you kibitzed. We kibitzed–talked–among ourselves in the social part of what came to be for me, "Friday night at the temple." Strangers had one thing in common–they practiced the same kind of Judaism. Some were more lax than others. Some led Seders that lasted longer, some tore off their challah pieces more haphazardly than others, but we all enjoyed the Oneg.

The rabbi's hands were raised when I blinked again. He had a delicate strength that prepared me for the angst of being a teen. Each week he gave me something to remember as I grew up awkwardly at home and dealt with bullies at school.

"May God bless you and keep you ..."

The rabbi was small in stature, but the tallis, the yarmulke and the raised hands created a giant on that bimah, the elevated stage at the head of the temple. After each nodding off, my eyes adjusted to the light and each time I was exponentially dwarfed by the giant Star of David on the ceiling. It was always surreal how the brown doors of the Ark drew shut, signaling a last chance for the week to glimpse the huge Torahs and their

elaborate velvety coverings and silver breast plates. This was the end–
the final, official end. Prayers had made their weekly nudge to people's
subconscious, an interesting sermon had been finely orated, homage had
been paid to Israel and God and the dead had been acknowledged. Blessing
us was the last thing on the rabbi's checklist.

The adolescent ritual had begun at sundown. It started at home on
Lyndale Avenue across form a Lutheran church. Most Fridays at home,
we observed the Sabbath. I felt fulfilled. We dropped a coin or two in a
cardboard Tzedakah box (charity) on the window ledge. A prayer book
was full of psalms for the evening. We shared the books. My dad always
read one with a dramatic flippancy. The prayer instructed us to bless our
mother, and for my dad to likewise praise her. It said she was a woman
of valor.

My sister and I stood up and said in unison "blessed" to our mom.
My dad, on his cue, quickly said, "Likewise I'm sure." The poem is very
sexist and chauvinistic, and, in retrospect, makes it all the more ironic we
said it, given we were a very liberal Reform family and gender equality
was one of our basic tenets. Commanded by the omniscience of our prayer
book, I turned my heart to my parents, a reciprocal gesture that became
incrementally less sincere. In the midst of my teenage recalcitrance these
sentiments were glibly exchanged between us in weekly prayer.

I was disobedient at fifteen, particularly to my dad, a fact that made it
all the more ironic that we said those words at that point in our relationship.
I was in the angst of adolescence, and often at odds with my dad. I thought
I knew it all.

Practically everything I've ever studied about Judaism can be traced
back to a tradition. There is a reason everything is done the way it is and

the origin is usually a compelling story. That always intrigued me. I was fascinated by how the traditions had been kept alive through centuries, at times compromising life itself. Our family practiced Reform Judaism which is based on choice through knowledge. My sister did not become a Bat Mitzvah until she was in her thirties, while most girls and boys (Bar Mitzvah) go through this rite of passage at thirteen. She did this by choice. She went to Hebrew school, though, as a child, and learned what is necessary to become a Bat Mitzvah. I was never inclined to study anything other than what was required to get myself through the public schools. That was hard enough for me and I think my parents knew that. Intellectually getting through high school was not hard, but in those years, because of my ethnicity, my physical ability and maybe being Jewish, I had too many personal issues on my plate.

I am Jewish because I was adopted by a Jewish family. My dad is German-Jewish and my mom descends from Russian Jews. By Orthodox Jewish law, because my biological mother is not Jewish, I am not truly Jewish. I would have had to have been converted and have accepted that conversion at age 13, but I think even without that, if I had wanted to become a Bar Mitzvah, I think I could have in our temple. In my adolescent years I embraced Judaism for good and bad. I liked its sense of uniqueness and cohesiveness and the way it gives you a definite identity. I accepted the stigma that being a Jew brings. By the late 1970s and early 1980s, Jews were not such a minority in Richfield, Minnesota. During the early '70s, though, we were one of a small handful of Jewish families in the suburb. Once a kid from a very Christian family—the kind whose mouth got a soapy taste when it swore—accused me of killing their savior. That was the first personal attack I remember. I think I took it to heart and really felt the cross Jews bear. I never did figure out how the blood of Christ made it from those little wine cups to my hands.

Many years later, on one of our Friday night temple sojourns, I witnessed public anti-Semitism for the first time. It was malicious and had the potential for serious danger. Not like a stupid kid or an ignorant adult who passive-aggressively asks for a more educated life. We approached our Reform synagogue–Temple Israel in Minneapolis–as a family for Sabbath services. Minimized by the enormity of the temple, a swastika was emblazoned on the walls. It was an indelible blemish on the place that in a light-handed way fulfilled a need in my life at that time.

Immediate reactions to hate crimes build indelible character. The arcane symbol of an Aryan nation tested my resolve like no bully ever had. It was like a giant black spider with venom to eradicate pockets of humanity. I wanted to know who had done that, who had acted out of insurmountable hatred, ignorance and inconsideration. Perhaps because of my dubious experience and ponders of the motives of bullies, I ultimately felt sorry for the perpetrators. I had learned early in life to consider the source, to consider from where bullies might come. These people were ignorant of Jews, of humanity in general, and were likely dissatisfied with their own lives. Rarely was my being Jewish the focus to bullies. I do not look Jewish as I am biracial and disabled which make being Jewish pale in comparison. Still, I can recall a few instances when a trifecta was reached. Slurs attacking all my handicaps found their way into the vast, derisive lexicon of my peers. That was clever indeed.

Boy Scouts was my compromise with tradition. I earned merit badges, each giving me a summarized course in a wide variety of practical life applications. I rose through the ranks of scouting: scout, tenderfoot, second class, first class, star, life. My parents could see I got something out of scouting and they encouraged me to pursue my Eagle, the highest ranking. I wore a sash across my chest displaying twenty-one merit badges at a ceremony November 2, 1983. Those badges, and a leadership project to benefit my community, earned me the rank of Eagle Scout. I was eighteen.

I went a step higher. After I earned my Eagle, I was recommended for the Order of the Arrow. It is an exclusive group in the boy scouts. Each member is said to be willing to "go the extra mile" for someone. The elders said it was a great honor to be selected. I never doubted them. The induction had an American Indian theme. Along the banks of the Rum River in Minnesota lies a camp where I, along with some of my fellow Eagle recipients, endured a weekend of self-discipline designed to test our character.

Ideally Jewish boys become Bar Mitzvahs at age thirteen. It is usually a part of the Sabbath service and the boy is called to read a small portion of the Torah. Tradition dictates that when the boy steps off the bimah, he is a man. A reception, similar to the Oneg, follows. It is regarded as a significant achievement and amply rewarded. The thirteen-year-old Bar or Bat Mitzvah receives material or monetary gifts from friends and relatives.

Scouting also poses a set of laws, which define how scouts are to live their lives. There are twelve, two of which are being obedient and reverent. At the time I was often disobedient and my reverence to anything was complicated by what was going on in my life. The acquisition of Eagle Scout teaches discipline much the way the study for a Bar Mitzvah does. Moving through the ranks, earning the merit badges and the final, charitable, Eagle project all require dedication that was usually hard for me to find at the time. I wanted to quit many times along the way, but my parents saw this was something attainable and pushed me. The closer I got to the award the more I knew it was something I wanted. It was something I could do right and be proud. I didn't do it because I thought it was expected and I had my parents' pride to win, I didn't do it because I knew I would get money–I did get $200– and I didn't do it to compete with my peers. It was my decision and I feel I am the better person for having done it.

Observing the Sabbath at home, tearing challah, blessing wine and reciprocally turning hearts from parent to child had a shelf life. Going to services Friday was something we did as a family in the late 1970s— coincidentally when the bullying of junior high was at its peak for me. My sister left for college in 1981 and Friday nights again became just the end of the school week. Peers of mine were all older and more mature— so the temple's timing was just right. Religion, the identity with a group and the commitment to something with more longevity than an Oneg Shabbat were all displayed to me in a way that left me options. I look back at those years and see what I am now because of them, how it made me more committed to family, how it taught me the responsibility of identifying with a group for better or worse and how it made me appreciate something even if it wasn't served on a silver pastry tray.

A Gentler Place

*T*he city kept on me. It cornered me by the hiss of my radiator and pestered me relentlessly. I looked across the hardwood floor from my roach-infested couch into the open bathroom. I admired the wide tub, perched on bear claw feet, and streamed consciousness of the generations of humans and roaches who had trod the boards. Steam rose from the radiator to obscure my sight, leaving me vulnerable to the city's ruse of luring me out of my apartment. Hindsight was better than I saw and on a subconscious level, every night as I lay awake, sirens wailed past my window. I invented ways to get out of that apartment. Friday was my escape from my mundane work persona. I grew fond of Brits, a British pub on the Nicollet Mall. I'd crossed the pond a couple of times and had grown accustomed to the homey atmosphere of a public house. They were gentler places where the proprietor welcomes you. The pub lacks bouncers who get paid to rush to judgments as they eye you and render their decision of whether you should be allowed to enter.

A colorful array of flags waved to me when I hopped off the bus–straight from work–at the corner of 11th and Nicollet. They all unfurled and brushed against one another. Union Jacks co-mingled with the fringes of Irish, Scottish and Welsh flags. I was greeted warmly at the door and ushered to a table for one. My waitress waited for me to return her flirtations. All the waitresses had tips in their eyes. I sensed none of them was interested in me from Adam. But it occurred to me that if I worked out on one routinely every Friday, I might establish some some kind of sincerity.

I drank my beer, waited on the fish and chips, and relished the chance for another pint. What now was a dinner had been a snack on the streets of Liverpool. They'd been pedestrian–giant slabs of battered cod coated in greasy smells and fermented in salt and vinegar. The slabs were wrapped tightly in a thick sheaf of newsprint. The cod I ate at Brits lacked the coarseness I found in England. The fish at Brits was tender and flaky and more suited for casual dining. The potato pieces were not chips either. They were the thick French fries that have become standard in American bars. The fish and chips were an expensive imitation. The pub crowd watched me as I set about soaking my fish in malt vinegar and sprinkled generous helpings of salt on the chips. Sometimes I went myself, other times I met friends. Usually no one showed up and I enjoyed the ambiance of anonymity as I dined. It was the setting for games. I wondered what their story was, or how significant was the expenditure of a fancy dinner and infinite pints to the common yuppie.

I assured myself that dropping twenty quid for dinner and two pints was insignificant. I had a disposable income. My attitude in those days was that I would work to enjoy myself and make my life easier. After treating myself with a spacious table for one, I went out beneath the stars, the tail lights of buses and the dawning of downtown's neon. I either caught a bus or hoofed the nine blocks home. If I opted for the latter, frequently I observed bums and winos fighting for a place to spend the night. They pawed at each other in their fingerless gloves, kicking last night's empty mouthwash containers. Sometimes drag queens lit up the night with their flamboyant fashion statements. There was a subdued look of discomfort for the fishnets and wigs they wore. If I bused, I acclimated to the stench of sweaty people with the glazed-over look of the junkie. I wagered they were going to their next drug deal, unnerved and indifferent to being shot.

♠

The city bus smelled like a liquor store. It careened back to the land of the 24-hour welfare check cashiers. There were pan-handlers that worked pedestrians with an aggressiveness that increased daily. I reached up instinctively and pulled the bus chord as we approached the DRUG FREE ZONE. I enjoyed the irony of the sign's directive. It warmed my heart to know that the city cared enough to post this subliminal message. It was sad, but it was the life some had chosen, or maybe they were the people life had chosen. The drug drill had been practiced enough so it was real and fulfilled their lives. They owned it outright. One fall evening, in the Steven's Community, a young junkie followed me when I got off the bus. The wind blew me along with the leaves to their guttural home. I quickened my pace to my apartment and the nefarious tradesman walked by me, trying to appear unconcerned a prospective enabler had eluded him. I watched his bony shoulders merely shrug in despair that yet another success had ignored his misery.

Actually, the crack house was just down the street from my Blackstone building. Cars passed the stately building, oblivious to the plight within its walls. The junkie's torn jeans, baggy, waist-shrinking concavity, ashen face and callow complexion drew attention away briefly from the monstrosity upon his shoulders. The toothless gummy smirk stained yellow, the between-crack snacks, obscuring the errant booze-breath that so begged for welfare, culminating in a frightful shock of stringy hair spilling from a black woolen cap.

I rounded the corner of my Blackstone building off 18th and Nicollet. I sighed and listened to the night. I heard the wind in the park wrap itself around one of the decadent signs, giving rise to the junkie's footsteps.

"Give me some money."

I refused to give him a dime and he wanted to fight. I told him to get a job. With no plausible answer, he squared off like a washed-out pug fighting for a life of drugs. I too took a stance, although no fight ensued and the miscreant skulked into the night, frustrated in his humiliation.

He hadn't hustled me; I stood my ground and upset his livelihood. So I remained cool, reeling slightly from the crack he made about fighting a handicapped person. Perhaps this is why he backed down. If I had actually beat him senseless, which wasn't my nature, could he have lived with himself? Could he have survived the daily thought of being overpowered by a handicapped person? I asked myself what should a person's disability have to do with it anyway? I was fit in those days. I lifted weights routinely. For all he knew—for all I knew—I might have easily won my first fight since junior high. It did trouble me that he had wasted his advantage over me. He had balance and dexterity. At the very least, this kid could find a job driving a cab. I had my own options, and that was an easy one I did not have.

I remember days like this;
When dew found the
Greenest hills my eyes can kiss
By a sun that
Followed Glasgow west to Larges;
I was vagrantly
Cool to streets of cobbled stone;

I recall days like this when
My backpack tore;
And my canvas shoes kicked
the dip sheep had left
As I climbed the hills to see
How far I had journeyed
From England to be estranged;

I remember days like this;
When I neared my
end and defied odds to miss
the undulated tongue
of Brogue spoke in twists;

I'll relish times wakes frayed
and Millport rain follows
the Hebrides' ferry mist;
I conquered all,
I swaggered streets to small
swelling shadowed risks
to toast at Midland pubs.

The Cheeky Lad

I get annoyed by phonies. In the end, I always find myself responding with impudence to people if they question my physical capacity. Authority figures need to be challenged. Bouncers, policemen, security guards–they've all heard the best of my impudence.

I pushed envelopes in my youth. If not for a head injury at age five and an adulthood cursed with an awkward gait and poor balance, questions such as "have you been drinking" would not arise. My walk mimics insobriety, and authority figures rush to conclusions. Beginning in high school and ending in college, I think I binge drank on the sub-conscious premise that my accusers would be validated. I could be sober and policemen insisted that I'd been drinking. My thought process (in my twenties) told me to load up on alcohol to make their suspicion real. That way, if they stopped me, arrested me, even threw me in jail for the night (which I came within a policeman's pinch of once), there would be grounds for their actions. I tested people's tolerance (and eventually mine) and acceptance. I enjoyed playing games with defiance.

£

In 1988 I went on a summer study program in England with the University of Minnesota-Duluth. We studied medieval English history at the University of Birmingham Monday through Thursday. The university had a pub and we'd congregate after class for several pints. The course consisted of touring the castles around Birmingham and Midlands. One field trip brought us to a fourteenth-century castle that was being excavated on the Welsh-English border. The schedule allowed us three-day weekends in which students, in individual groups, would travel all over the United Kingdom. I, however, usually by choice, traveled alone.

Our class, comprising students from colleges all over the United States, became well acquainted at the university's pub. After we were sufficiently high, the group walked (I took a cab) to go "have a curry" at one of the many Indian restaurants around Birmingham. However, Thursday nights ended differently. Following our pub time and subsequent curry, with my rail pass I boarded a train bound for a randomly chosen UK destination. Location was not important– spontaneity, adventure, pushing envelopes were.

One weekend, Scotland's Hebrides called to me. I wanted to get to the sea. I chose a place that I was sure no one in my group would be going to. I wanted to gaze out over the Atlantic once during my two-week stay in the land-locked Midlands of England. I headed as far west as I could get on the train. The main British rail system took me to Glasgow. From there I took a commuter train to Larges on Scotland's coast. I looked at a map and chose the tiny isle of Millport. The ferry docked and I looked around, admiring my latest conquest, slightly surprised that my intentions had worked out for me.

£

In a khaki-colored, tattered, ill-fitting raincoat and a black corduroy "Lennon" cap, I trudged into town. My thin, frayed, nylon day pack and canvas sneakers were of little value in the maritime climate. I'd read about horses to view and possibly ride. Finding them became an obsession. I trembled in my remote vagrancy. I had a sense from past experience that I was pushing an envelope and I may have to account to some authority figure for my ataxic unbalanced gait. The sense wedged itself like a shiv in the back of my mind.

The rain increased and I doubled my pace, putting my canvas sneakers to the test. Finally, I spotted a barn where I thought horses must be.

"Excuse me, I was told in Larges that there are some horses to ride on the Island."

"Aye, Larges. Ferry take you out here laddy?"

"Yes," I nodded, wondering how else I would arrive in this tiny world.

"You're American, are ye lad?"

"Of course I am," I shot back, not really thinking that my dark complexion might lead someone to think I was from a Latin country.

"Aye, so you are."

The heavy brogue I heard was barely decipherable. I knew it was English, but still very hard to understand. It had a musical quality that was fun. I listened to catch where the accented syllable went. I smiled, realizing that I was in a part of the UK where I was sure my able-bodied classmates would not come. Through the raindrops, peering from the greenest grass on this earth, I spotted what appeared to be the ruins of a castle. The sound of splashing tires interrupted the desolation. A man in a running suit and his uniformed flunky wanted to know what I was doing there, voicing concern that I might be lost. Again the thick brogue presented me with amusement and I felt at the very least I could tell about this back at the pub.

streets of Millport

I explained what I was doing in the UK, trying to display my best attempt to appear the able-bodied tourist. I sensed my sobriety was in question. At first the two men used the pretense that I was a vagrant, after which the older man in the jogging suit asked me if I had recently consumed any alcohol or drugs. I was impudent; not realizing American democracy was not around to protect my rights. (I later learned that under Scottish law I could be held under suspicion and brutalized. Basically I was guilty until proven innocent.) The two men forced me into the back of their van. I vented my anger by convincing myself I was happy just to be out of the rain. We arrived at a small stone structure. I sat across a table from the middle-aged man in the jogging suit while the younger uniformed man stood by trying to intimidate me. I relaxed and put my feet on the table. I thought if these men were truly looking out for my welfare, I would take full advantage of their hospitality.

"Could I have a spot of tea then?" I asked in my best aristocratic English accent.

The bloke in the jogging suit frowned and asked for my ID and passport.

"Read me your ID," the man demanded as I placed the requested passport and state ID before him.

"What's the matter, can't you read?" I boldly asked. He shot me a look of contempt and reached for the phone. I can only assume he called the University of Birmingham to ask if any of its students was in Millport. He hung up the phone, looked at his uniformed inferior and then at me. He grunted "Aye, you're a cheeky lad," and waved me off like an annoying fly. I smiled again, for I had won. I had pushed the envelope all the way to their tiny village and was called cheeky. In an unsettlingly rebellious way, the exoneration and pronouncement from a middle-age constable in a jogging suit (likely on his day off) made the trip worth everything. I had bucked a foreign system—not a democracy. It had always provided a good rush in the States, but it was twice as good on a remote island in the Hebrides.

I stumbled out of the stone structure a falsely accused deviant. I realized then that I resented the constables also for taking me out of my way. They had greatly inconvenienced me by questioning me, and then leaving me to find the ferry again from the backstreets of Millport. I walked back in the station angered.

"How do I get back to town?" Constructive help was not given. I figured it might be since they were so concerned for my well-being. What if I never made it off the island? If I missed the last ferry and never made it back to Birmingham? What if I did not show up in class Monday? I could hold Scotland Yard liable, bring them to trial and cause an international incident. I could sue Millport and bankrupt the tiny town. How much money could they have? Scenarios went around in my head while I wandered the slim cobbled backstreets of Millport. Rain, real or the lingering vestiges of it, had dampened any spirits I had brought from England.

Staring from the back of the ferry to Larges, I watched the wake spike scenarios of where I'd been. I saw things through the caged window of a police van and I felt the smug eyes of the man in the jogging suit as he belligerently conceded that I was a cheeky lad. When the ferry docked I bolted down the gang plank. I felt the wet flimsiness of my canvass sneakers. I did not care that my socks were beginning to dampen and I walked adamantly east into town. I listened to them squish over the bleats that rose from the dots of woolly plumage. Soon I was running up into the lush, green hills, my soaked canvas sneakers collecting sheep dip.

Exercising Demons

Chronic ataxia is a deficiency in muscle coordination. In my case it was the result of a head injury. On January 8, 1971, a car driven by a distracted 17-year old tapped my fragile skull. Three weeks shy of my sixth birthday, I entered a six week coma. During this time I received therapy to keep my muscles from atrophying. My face contorted. It twisted as I writhed in pain. I was discharged from the hospital on March 11.

Soon a physical therapist was hired to come to the house. She'd begin my therapy wherever she found me. In the beginning, much of my therapy consisted of scores of excruciatingly painful abdominal exercises. Finally the ability to sit upright (precariously) was regained. Rehabilitative walks with my dad comprised the next four years.

By the spring of 1975 I was standing with the help of wooden crutches. My dad thought I was ready for a new challenge. It was time for a new interest, something we could do together. We watched the documentary *Pumping Iron* starring Arnold Schwarzenegger, Lou Ferrigno, Franco Columbu and all the bodybuilders who made the sport popular. I was hooked. What I saw appealed to me, and I thought it was something I could do. Being a Mr. Olympia or Mr. Universe was probably not in the cards though.

My challenge began when I acquired a fifty pound barbell. We set aside an hour every night to do exercises out of a book. My dad was very methodical, scrutinizing an exercise and executing it with great precision. I watched him and performed the exercise to the best of my ability. He never expected me to be able to do them at his level of perfection. He knew my capabilities, but he also knew that if he didn't push me some, I probably would not push myself.

My dad's big cast-iron weights, all black and shiny, made my small, maroon, twenty-five pound discs look like toys. He put 30 pounds on each end of a six-foot bar he had found in our attic. My bar was four-feet long, brand new, and came with a set of dumbbells. A hex wrench tightened the screws on the small iron collars at each end of the bar. His had bigger, bell-shaped collars that tightened simply by turning the extended handle.

We took turns "spotting" each other. Still having the precarious balance of a tight-rope-walker and the gait of a three-legged man, I braced myself over my dad to spot him. The reality was that I was likely ineffective as a spotter. Even so, he was always careful not to diminish my confidence.

§

In the fall of 1977 I entered junior high. Being different and defenseless made me a target for bullies. It put a fire in me that manifested itself in misdirected anger and, at times, recalcitrance. My workouts began in the tiny weight room of the school. The air was stagnant and dry. A bitter-sweet sweated smell intruded on my nose and fed that fire like oxygen. I grew accustomed to the scent and a desire to rise above, or at least gain, the bullies' respect flourished. Dimly lit and uninspiring, the junior high weight room consisted of a rusted Universal machine, a few dumbbells and a sit-up board. It was crude, but adequate for someone beginning training. Pent-up anger poured into the weights. I felt good about myself and it gave me confidence and self-esteem. The weight room became a haven from bullies.

Eventually I craved something bigger. A friend and I rode our bikes a half mile every day after school to the YMCA. I never measured myself up against anyone. I never worried about what they were doing or what they thought I should be able to do. One thing I learned early on: If you want to get anywhere in weight training, your ego has no place. You must be secure. If my peers took notice, great; if not, all the more reason to work harder. Physically I think deep down I knew that I could never be their equal, but I thought a few muscles and a show of discipline might someday earn their respect.

I tried to keep a low profile in the Y's weight room. However, with a crutch in hand, that is a difficult task. My friend, who was deadly serious about his routine, went his own way. We rarely lifted together. The biggest obstacle for me was enduring the judgmental, condescending, or heroic reactions of the other lifters. They praised me for my diligence. I was not worthy of their praise. Why did they even care? I was tempted to tell them to take their praise and. . .give it to someone who wants or needs it. They talked down to me, like I was not in there to lift seriously, like my able-bodied friend for example. Some were full of training tips and others just stared.

"There he is," I heard in a patronizing voice."

Or some were compelled to instruct me, just assuming I hadn't a clue of what I was doing.

"You shouldn't lift that way," or "you're not breathing right."

It was worthy advice for a beginning lifter. Maybe it was something I would say, but only if I were asked. A question nagged at me though: Would they be giving someone tips if a crutch was not in sight? In fact, I noticed a few other novices, some even younger than myself and no one ever welcomed them or gave them instructions. Generally, though, either they did not understand me or I did not understand their compliments and backhanded advisories. Or maybe their need to stack their own egos. But even if that were the case, why me? There were plenty of young kids looking like they knew less than I did. Why weren't they adopted to be the grass hopper to the sensei?

Eventually the Young Men's Christian Association became boring to us. We had each reached a plateau. My friend entertained thoughts of competitive bodybuilding. At that point, I just wanted to train like those guys in *Pumping Iron*. I was satisfied with how my plan had worked with the bullies. The confidence in myself was enough–then. Both of us–for differing reasons–needed to be surrounded by people who were as serious as we were. We began biking even further after school to a place simply called "The Gym."

A hot-house air was moist and caressed my face. It was the adrenaline charging sweated smell I had learned so often in the small, rudimentary junior high weight room. I was home. I proudly walked into the gym on my own two feet. It was an early graduation. The eclectic smell now included Ben-Gay. Iron weight plates made a loud *clank* when they were added to a bar. It was the sound of progress. What I heard was intense and focused. No one talked or stared. Every nuance of the gym sounded honest. Every feeling was owned and echoed the aspirations of each individual. Great bowls of chalk sat on tall pedestals. They were usually half-full. White residue from grips released and hands clapped in encouragement coated the floors. Mirrors looked on with faces lined in pain. The images were of men and women heaving weights and grimacing their best productive pain. They lifted correctly, extracting everything a movement had to offer. Egos were not at stake there. If they were, they usually were not by the next week. The ones who stayed did not "cheat" like I had seen so much at the YMCA and voluntarily call muscles into action not intended to be exercised. There were no personal trainers or motivators. It was everyone's objective in that gym to get big. The bodybuilding stage was their goal. Massive muscles rippled out of sweat-soaked shirts and showed me where I wanted to go.

My friend meticulously recorded his amounts of weight, number of sets and number of repetitions in a notebook. With less discipline and a margin for error, I did the same. He went through more books than I did. At times we compared notes to see what was working and what wasn't. He took a very methodical approach to lifting. My friend had all the bodybuilding books. He followed the routines of bodybuilders who were currently reigning and subscribed to *Muscle & Fitness*.

"Don't talk to me," he said during our workouts at the gym.

I never did. We encouraged one another. He knew what I was running from and I knew where he wanted to go.

Our house was down the street from the high school. Finally I could walk to school. I was physically a little bigger and my school mates were mentally a little bigger. No one bullied me anymore. The high school had a much bigger weight room. I was in the "early risers" club and worked-out before school. I always noticed the sign at the door that read: Wishing Won't Work, Working Will. The subliminal message of that sign worked itself in my mind.

§

By 1991 I thought I should take my pursuit to the next level; competitive bodybuilding. After half-hearted lifting and poor diets through five years of college, I was the fattest I'd ever been. At 5 feet 7 inches, I weighed almost 220 pounds. I had at least 50 pounds of body fat to lose.

My job at the time was very physically demanding. I worked out five days a week and ate six small, low-fat meals a day. Pounds flew off and muscle started to make an appearance. But I was burning more calories than I was consuming, which is not good in order to build muscle. The objective to "cutting up" is to lose the lighter weight of body fat while retaining the heavier weight of skeletal muscle. I upped my caloric intake. Eating enough (of the right things) is not as easy as it sounds.

I began my diet in the late spring of 1993. By September I had that "ripped" look for competition. Muscles hold their shape and the skin is solid to the touch. My energy felt abundant with so little fat to carry. It is a great way to be. With my gait, which has been described by doctors as awkward, the less dead weight to carry the better. Maybe some of my friend's methodology had rubbed off on me. I was lean and had followed a diet for three months. It was harvest time. I went online and filled out an entry form. I printed it out and sent it in to the NPC (National Physique Committee). I just wanted to compete a little, perhaps be in contention with an individual. My able-bodied competitors were professional aspirants. They were all bigger, had the coordination to pose well and had the symmetry that is so crucial to bodybuilding. I have a left hemiparesis. This partial paralysis renders the muscles on my left side generally unresponsive to conditioning.

At one of the NPC shows I could at least say I was natural. My competitors were freakishly big and steroids coursed through their veins. Muscles on steroids are like balloons blown beyond their natural inflated size. That was sickening to me. They were cheating not just me but themselves as well. The closest I ever came to using any kind of performance enhancer was the brief use of a fat burner called ephedrine. As I recall, it was eventually taken off the market. My trainer said I did not need it, and my metabolism was fast enough to burn fat.

The NPC competitions took place at local high school auditoriums mostly. I tried not to let my confidence waver. Walking down the halls of the high school I sized up my competition. Sharp jaw lines leveled my eye. Not feeling like they'd edge me out of competition before I stepped on stage was impossible. Smudgy, tan-painted faces hid behind rice cakes. Some looked like they were coming from—or going to—fight in a jungle. Their faces were worn with a look of depletion. (In the final week you gradually deplete your body of carbohydrates followed by a 24-hour period of dehydration.) In the topical tanning agents swam a bewilderment that was punctuated by crumbs of rice cake. Baggy "zubas," and sweat pants ensconced chiseled quadriceps. Those over-stuffed sweat shirts I had seen at The Gym now hung looser with tight muscle. It was impossible not to second guess myself. These guys were huge! My confidence took a beating.

Getting to the stage and training hard and natural is the most fun for me. I thrived on the challenge the competitions offer. In the back of my mind I think I knew then that I really did not have an honest chance of winning anything against able-bodied athletes.

"Are you having fun?" the promoter asked as I came off stage.

It was said in the same patronizing register the guy at the YMCA had used. To be honest, the promoter was exactly right, although I have to say part of me was frustrated that no one saw me as a serious competitor. Was it so inconceivable that I might actually beat someone? I had no real expectations of winning but could I place and not just show? It burned me that the concept of someone with a disability actually excelling seemed foreign to them. I was always dead last. I once took a copy of the judge's score sheet just to see this on paper. It was a bitter pill to swallow.

§

In the winter of 1996 I was in a health club when a bodybuilder told me of an organization that had divisions for "physically challenged" athletes, those in a wheelchair and those who were able to stand. The ABA (Amateur Bodybuilding Association) is a California-based organization that has divisions for everyone regardless of age or ability. I could now really compete and, ostensibly, I could win. Invigorated by the doors now open to me, I trained harder for a New York competition in the summer of 1997.

For the next six years I competed with the ABA, choosing one or two shows a year around the country. Only once did the ABA promote a show in my own state of Minnesota. In 2001 I flew to Hawaii to compete in the ABA natural Olympia and brought home a gold medal. Except for that one, my dad went to every show. He was there supporting me, rewarding my victories or consoling my defeats.

34

My dad and me at a 2002 show

I really felt like a contender, like those guys in *Pumping Iron*. A guy with cerebral palsy became my chief competitor. We were always in contention, he and I, and often came within a point or two of each other. A morning pre-judging is where most of the decisions are made. You line up with the others in your class and are instructed by a panel of judges to hit certain poses. "Front-double biceps, rear lat spread," or "side triceps," they asked politely to see. We did our best. I often tried to get in my opponent's head. I distracted them or smiled down the line at them, patronizing them like I once was.

evening show-Las Vegas, 2004

The evening show was, for the most part, a formality. Beautiful women, all dressed to the hilt, milled around the trophy table. The female bodybuilders backstage were an attraction to me, but the evening show was both emotionally grueling and enticing. I did my little routine–a few dumbbell flys or push ups–to pump blood to the muscles. Or, sometimes, another competitor held out a towel and I tried to pull it away from him. I pulled it in to my chest with both hands, thereby pumping up my latissimus muscles. The idea was to get that "winged" look. Competitors emerged from the wings of the stage keeping their arms bowed. I watched all the glamour and let the music and applause at the end of each individual posing routine work its magic. It did, and when my class was called I was totally immersed in the show

The music began, music for which I had perfected a routine. I hit poses that were *my* favorites, not the judges'. The audience grew louder with each pose.

This, in itself, was a drug, a performance enhancer. After my class—PC standing—was through, we might be called back. All five of us came out on stage to settle a score, a contention that could be altered by the tweak of a muscle. (I did this at the 2001 natural Olympia and won gold. I actually flexed my biceps and tweaked the top.) The pose down was the pinnacle of competition to me. It did not get better than that. I loved the camaraderie and adulation—the final reward for all the hours in the gym. And you knew your first full meal of hedonistic proportions was coming soon. It was usually done to loud trendy music that shook the rafters. We struck poses timed to the beats. We smiled frantically and toed a line on the stage with our feet. It was the mark from the morning and we all vied to be first. Then the beautiful women in evening gowns hung medals around our necks. The trophies were always awarded in ascending order. "Third place. . .second place." That left first anti-climactic. With the ABA physically challenged I won some. I placed in a few. I always was able to do more than just show.

Las Vegas- October, 2002

Ramifications of Schadenfreude

louds can obscure the sun when random individuals go looking for divine intervention. Often, the most ordinary lives must be shaken. They'll wait in their complacent cages that yearn to be rattled. Sometimes a man will spend his whole life looking for an out, a crossroads to a less mundane existence. He'll call for an intervention.

Aaron had briefly known about a life he might have led. Had fate conspired differently he would not have been in that car, speeding toward BSU for his sophomore year as a sociology major. He went into his second year with knowledge attained from the adoption agency. In the brief description of Aaron's biological father's pursuits and interests sociology had been listed. Like Aaron, he played chess. The records also indicated that his biological father was a SCUBA diver; Aaron had become certified as an open water diver a few years ago.

The coincidences intrigued him. It was as if Aaron had met his father years ago when he stumbled through a paternal vortex sequestered in mirrors. He enjoyed the speculative nature of this theory. He knew though that it was simply the work of deoxyribonucleic acid. Aaron played chess and liked to dive because of tiny twisted molecular structures on a twisted helix.

"What would you think if I decided to find my biological parents?" Aaron asked Shirley, his mother since he was two weeks old.

"How long have you wanted to do this?"

"Actually my roommate Ron gave me the idea. He's adopted and had no interest in ever finding his parents. I can't believe him," he looked in the rear-view mirror for validation, "I just want you and Dad to know that whatever happens, I will still love you the same."

"That's very considerate of you. No, I'm fine; I can't speak for your father though." Mrs. Sullivan sighed. She gave her son a consoling look,

"I just hope you know the risk you're taking. You could go through a long search and wind up getting a door slammed in your face."

"I know. There are some great stories of adopted kids finding their parents and some that end horribly. A girl in high school went looking for her biological parents. She had a door slammed in her face and then she was disowned by her adoptive parents."

"Don't worry, that won't happen to you. Whatever happens, we'll be there for you."

"Well, thanks, I guess. I appreciate it, but I really didn't think there'd be much chance of that happening. Agencies make all the contacts now and the worst that can happen is I get a nasty letter."

"What if they trick you? You know, lead you into thinking they want to see you. Then, when you've traveled to meet them, they dash your hopes and slam the door on you."

He looked at her strangely, wondering why she was filling his head with such malicious thoughts.

"Why in the world would they do anything like that?" he asked.

"Your biological parents were very likely forced into placing you for adoption. Perhaps they've resented for years having to make that decision. A vindictive part of them might take it out on you. You were adopted by a couple who never had to make such decisions. The biological parents might have been poor and had to struggle to make ends meet. They resent the life we gave you that they couldn't. They're going to see a child who takes it for granted that their past is there with an open door and a welcoming smile." Aaron saw his mother's social work skills in action.

"Oh, I'll be careful. I'll know whether I'm welcome."

"Oh, I see," she conceded, "you have it all planned out, you've weighed the consequences?"

"Mom, I have to do this," Aaron said pounding the dashboard. "I still think Ron really wants to do something like this. Maybe seeing me do this will change his mind."

"No, don't get into it with him. He may really not care to know. I think you have more faith than he does."

He stared out the window and watched the green and red lights of the shipping trade on Lake Superior. They sparkled in the distance and Aaron thought of all adopted kids who had to find their roots. Aaron turned to his mother with a quizzical look.

"You're messin' with me. Somewhere in his sub-conscious I know Ron has a need for some kind of closure. Everyone needs to meet their biological mother at least once in their life."

"Aaron, do you and Ron ever talk about this?"

"He'll always try to change the subject. He usually has some backward way of bringing it up though. He'll delicately steer the conversation there, but retreat as it nears. I think he really wants to talk about it."

The drizzle outside prodded Aaron, turning his origin into an obsession. It tapped on the car's windows like a porter hired to take him and his baggage to their destination. Aaron looked to his roommate for guidance. He considered Ron his only real friend at Bixby State.

"You remember that day after graduation when Dad took Phil, Dan, and me up here? They deserted me," he threw his up hands. "But, you know, if they had come here I wouldn't have even tried to make any friends at Bixby. I probably would have just hung with them. So, I guess I'm glad they bailed out on me.

Ω

The documents from the adoption agency described Aaron's biological father as "hesitant in initiating friendships." Bixby State University was a small campus. Bixby, Minn., was a quiet town of 800 on the fringe of the Iron Range. He reasoned that by minimizing the population, he increased his chances of being randomly chosen for something.

"Are you going to be coming home next weekend?"

"I don't know for sure. I'll give you a call early in the week if I do."

Aaron had selected a "suitcase college." BSU offered little in the way of social clubs. Keg parties in open-pit mines and off-campus houses were the social stimulants. Dancing at dingy clubs also entertained the handful of students who stayed on the weekends. The lure of the beer keg was strong at BSU and Aaron had succumbed to it his first weekend as a freshman. Thursday evenings the sound of trunks slamming and engines starting echoed through the Commons.

"You know, a few weeks ago, the registrars raised the issue of holding Friday classes again. Ron campaigned against it. He argued that by not having Friday classes, he could go home and work and afford to go to school here."

"Were his reasons considered?"

"I doubt it, but he likes to think they were."

"So were Friday classes re-instated?"

"Yes, but he schedules his classes so he can leave Thursday night."

"Doesn't that limit his choices?"

"Sure it does. He doesn't care, he's a rebel. He has his own little world and if the college doesn't jibe with it he won't jibe with them."

"Sounds to me like Ron has security issues."

Aaron pictured Ron in his mother's private practice someday finally discovering who he was. Mrs. Sullivan carefully deposited Aaron's small bag under his bunk, gazing curiously at the top one. All the times she had been there the upper bunk was covered with a faded, green sleeping bag. It was clear to Mrs. Sullivan that Ron needed to exhibit his flippant attitude of school. On the desk next to Aaron's was a notebook and a few pens in perfect alignment.

"Boy, Ron really clears out of here. You barely know he's coming back."

Aaron laughed, "I had a girl in here once. She saw the sleeping bag and asked if my roommate was an exchange student. He'll be back tonight though."

"Oh, maybe you can arrange to ride home with him sometime."

"I'll ask him, but he's kind of a loner."

Mrs. Sullivan kissed her son and left the room. He stood there deciding whether to unpack, eat at the cafeteria, study or find an open door in the dorm. People always left their doors open.

Ω

"How was the weekend?"

"All right, nothing too exciting. I got over eighty hours in at the job," Ron smiled as he put a few new pens in his desk. He was always alluding to a secret life that was most likely nefarious. He'd present himself as a scrupulous, diligent, young college student and then leave each Thursday to a clandestine life. "Whole Foods is paying me more than they should. They have no idea, and what they don't know won't hurt them," he said grinning smugly.

"You know Ron, it might catch up to you someday. You'll owe all that money back and I'll be laughing."

"Ah, I'm not too worried about it. You'd do the same thing if you were in my shoes, right?"

Ron was balding at thirty-eight. He explained once that college had been a late decision. After high school Ron had went to work stocking food and gradually worked his way up to assistant produce manager. When he felt he had enough tenure–enough that terminating him for embezzlement wasn't likely–he decided to pick a real career.

He had a thick, orange mustache and small blue rodent-like eyes. He was kind of a weasel and masterfully crossed the passivity of a rabbit with the aggression of a ferret. Aaron looked at his roommate as a pathetic puppeteer, in command of all his puppet's strings yet master of none of them. Aaron sat at his desk, stretching his feet out as he leaned back in his swivel chair.

"Actually no, I wouldn't. I would not want to come down here each week and worry about returning to a splattered wall."

"Splattered wall?"

"That one went right over your head, not that there's much up there to stop it."

"Oh, that was clever. What did you mean?" Ron's tiny blue eyes grew beadier.

"Splatters usually happen when something hits a fan." Aaron leaned back further and folded his hands behind his head. Ron shrugged, knowing this argument was lost.

"Almost time for *M*A*S*H,*" said Aaron. "You gonna watch it?"

"Yeah, yeah, don't worry," he scoffed as he uncoiled the cord of his small portable TV. "There, knock yourself out." Ron picked up a notebook and some pens from his desk. "I'm going to the study lounge."

Aaron grabbed a soda out of his small refrigerator he'd received as a graduation gift and settled in to watch his favorite show. It was the only program for which Ron took his TV out of its little corner on the top shelf of his closet. Every night, precisely at six o'clock, occasionally a moment before, Ron took down the only permanent thing in his closet. The small, portable set stayed in the closet all weekend. It was symbolic of the game Ron played with BSU. He merely humored it and his suppressed ambitions with his patronage. He spoke of his blue-collar existence often to justify that patronage. He'd never embrace life or show any evidence of his curiosity in its perplexities. Ron was like a born-again Christian who didn't surrender his life to Christ. He was simply born-again—and then again each weekend. He transcended nothing but the college registrars and his employer. Like the Christians claimed to be, Ron was *in* the world and not *of* it. Whatever he was born-again as would most likely never be discovered or rewarded; deified or canonized. He never missed an opportunity to flog the world–or those who tried to get closer to enjoying life–with apathy and mockery. In short, he protested too much.

Ω

"Hello, this is Aaron Sullivan."

"This is Mari Whiting with the Sheltering Limbs Adoption Agency. You may remember you and your mother met with me a year ago. You told me then that you wanted us to locate your father."

The black man and white woman who'd conceived Aaron twenty years ago were never married. It ended abruptly when his conception was brought to the man's attention.

Aaron's heart raced. Dozens of scenarios had gone through his mind in the past year.

"I-I did, I mean I chose him over my mother," he said, swallowing hard as he realized that he may have chosen the wrong parent.

"Yes you did back in October. We obtained a copy of a driver's license and a call was placed. A woman answered." Mari conveyed the findings in a cold and sterile manner as if it were in a police report. The warm and optimistic feeling from the previous year had disappeared. "He could not be reached for comment. So we ran a search for your biological mother. Your biological father left her and she gave birth to you alone. She considered raising you herself, possibly with the help of her mother but decided it would be hard on you. She decided giving you up for adoption would be best. Her name is Jane Swenson.

"I can't believe it. Do you know how many times I've thought about this call? Here it is now and I haven't a clue what to say. I'd better sit down." He felt his heart palpate the cotton of his shirt as the receiver involuntarily dropped to the floor. "I'm sorry about that, just a bit overwhelmed."

"That's quite all right Aaron," she said, resuming the warm manner he recalled.

"So, what's next for me?"

"Well," Mari calmly began, "you should be receiving a letter from Jane in a few weeks. I gave her your address at home, the one you and Shirley gave me. Is that all right or do you want her to send it to you there in Bixby?"

"Is that possible?"

"It would mean another phone call. There is a fee for each contact we make," she explained, minimizing its importance the best she could. Aaron thought of the money he had already spent. He could not put a price on this.

"Yes, please have her send it here."

"Very well Aaron," Mari said politely, reassuring him of a timely response.

Ω

"Hey Ron, back so soon?"

"Yeah, couldn't really get into it. What's up with you? You look like you're in a daze, even for you."

"You noticed. How special that you note things like that at your advanced age."

"Funny. What's up?"

"That was the woman from my adoption agency. Guess she contacted my biological mother. She said she was very receptive to the call."

"But I thought you wanted to find your old man first, you know, the black part of you?"

"They tried contacting him. He was not receptive at all, if it was even him."

"What? Do you think they're putting you on? Look, Aaron, if he didn't want you then, what's going to change so much in all that time?" Aaron sat down, switched off the TV and shrugged as he fell back into his chair. He really had no answer that would satisfy Ron, let alone himself. Maybe all the negativity Ron brought to this subject was the prudent thing to do. To be overly optimistic here could really have long-term consequences.

"Look, man, you never tried. Personally, I think you're scared. I don't know, maybe I did get my expectations up too high. It's just something I need to know, okay."

"Are you sure you really *need* to know it, or just *think* you need to know it," Ron pondered innocently.

"Oh Lord, what are you getting at now?"

"Well, I just think it's worth examining what really motivated you to do this. I was adopted when I was a year old. My old man sat me down and told me straight out when I was about fifteen. I remember it well. But he made it sound like I'd regret it if I thought about things too much."

Ron was a very closed person. The few acquaintances he allowed into his BSU world he kept at arm's length. The friends he had at college were from his hometown. He looked much older than he was, and peers regularly reminded him of it. His indifferent collegiate peers heaped insults on him as though he were a superman, emotionally speaking. Ron waltzed in and out of BSU each week mocking the students who were really serious. He never really let reality touch him. He never let himself face the things that might hurt him.

"Did it ever occur to you that your dad was covering himself? The truth may have been that he couldn't handle your trying to find your biological parents."

"Look, they adopted me. Who am I to question that? To me, it would be a slap in the face if my kid all of a sudden went off looking for his *real* parents," Ron said, raising his fingers to make quotations. "You should know that. Didn't you declare sociology as your major? I know sociology deals with humans as they act in a group, but you must have some insight into the individual."

"No. I'm not sure now. Thanks a lot. And by the way, it's not 'all of a sudden.' Leave it to you to spoil things."

"What did I do?"

"Why did you have to remind me that he was my first choice? I was so happy about hearing from my mother. Now you have me thinking about the reasons he did not even come to the phone to talk to the agency woman. I think his wife answered the phone. Now you have me thinking I have half-siblings out there somewhere. Suppose he's protecting something. Consciously or subconsciously he wants to bury me. Maybe he was raised where people think it's mortal sin to have a child out of wedlock–let alone as an interracial couple."

Aaron speculated on possible scenarios Miss Whiting had never approached. In their meeting last year Aaron had noticed the absence of a ring on her finger. She was an attractive, single social worker who had no clue of what a wife might do if a husband's illegitimate son suddenly called out of the blue. For all either of them knew–Aaron or Mari–his father and his wife had produced his half-siblings and were one big happy family.

"C'mon, let's go get some pizza. You know, celebrate your good fortune. Well, hopefully."

"Why? Are you buying?"

"Why would I buy? Who do you think I am, Rockefeller? Every nickel I make goes to BSU for my imminent career in espionage," he chuckled shrewdly.

Ω

Somehow surviving in spite of its sparse patronage, McVie's existed in anonymity across College Street. The pizza was doughy, greasy and had more crust than anything else. The proximal location of the eatery may have contributed to the fact that it, like the college, really offered nothing in the way of socialization. Because BSU was a "suitcase college," no one really spent enough time there to form any kind of club. Students either packed into the run-down dance club a mile from campus or went home on the weekends. Aaron was a regular at Driscols, the club downtown. Every

Friday or Saturday night that he stayed on campus, or both, he marched off campus down to Driscols with implacable purpose.

In 1985 Morris Day and the Time punctuated the rhythms of the night. A song called "The bird" and Prince's "I would die for U" layered venues in which college kids got crazy. "Purple Rain," or Spandau Ballet's "True" was the king of slow-dance songs and Aaron made the trek to Driscols most weekends hoping to hear it. His contentment craved stillborn inebriation and the soft waist of a co-ed. He went to his club in raging snow, at times in defiance of Shirley's warnings. Driscols was Aaron's escape from the reality of the college world, although it was this world into which he had willingly thrust himself. High school was over too fast and life was upon him. College was the next step in Aaron's hierarchy of mediocrity. It was an institution one might be allowed to marinate in before tasting what was presumably a sweet life. It was surely this ambivalence that drove Aaron to college and then to debase himself weekly at Driscols. Ron never made it down to Aaron's refuge. He had a life back home, even if all it consisted of was punching a clock. His life though was panning out better than Aaron's. He secretly envied Ron's subtle, unassuming, blue-collar approach to the American dream. That, or whatever life had in its coffers that decade. In the grand scheme of most ambitious peoples' lives, Ron was content to be a spectator in life. He didn't need to know everything and, reciprocally, his life proved less complicated. Simply put, Ron did not ask too much of it. He was happy to go home to his job, let the boss put him on the night shift, possibly fool payroll, return to college and entertain himself with *M*A*S*H*, a show that often displayed the lighter side of war.

"Hey, how's Driscols been?"

"Oh, it's there. Nothing too exciting."

"How are the women down there?"

"Fine, but sort of flaky. Occasionally you run into one that has her feet on the ground and an idea in her head."

"Are you sure you don't go down there just to *put* ideas in their heads?"

Aaron sat spinning his thumbs around a string of cheese, staring at the pizza as if it were an oracle. "Maybe I do Ron, or maybe I don't. We'll never know now will we?"

"Com'on man, don't' play innocent with me. I've heard people talk about the women that put you to bed. It sounds like you turn our room into a brothel when I leave. I don't care. Just never let any of 'em get anything on my bunk, okay?"

Aaron nodded in quiet humility as his image as a playboy was plucked from his grips. He heard commendations about his exploits and that was fine; he liked that. Somehow, though, he needed Ron's assessment of him to be clear of his weekend debasement. Ron nonchalantly extolled a work ethic, thumbing his nose at authority while reaping all its benefits. Usually he arrived back for class Monday morning, expediting the two-hour drive perfectly. Save for the times his Buick hit a deer, Ron pulled into BSU's parking lot in plenty of time to casually saunter into class. So relaxed was he that once he had a pizza ordered ahead of time.

"Aaron, you know that time I said I stopped to order a pizza on the way back here? Well the guy came into class with the pizza, looked around anxiously and I say, 'Right here dude.' Now is that funny or what?"

"I guess it is mildly amusing. You really don't get why we're here do you?"

"Where, BSU?"

"No Einstein, why we're in this life."

Ron rolled his eyes in anticipation of the philosophical musings he heard all too often from his roommate. His lack of comfort became apparent and Ron fidgeted with whatever he could. He seized control of the discussion in an attempt to evade its stated purpose or just exited the room without so much as a nod. Aaron loved to put Ron's blistering feet closer to the irons. He knew that underneath that cool, apathetic charm lurked a curious man. As he saw it, his job was to exploit this person for all its worth.

"Look my friend, don't drag me into your world. I'm happy right here learning my trade and makin' a few bucks off the man. It's people like you with their head in the clouds and their nose turned up that I could really do without!"

Aaron angrily wiped his mouth with a fistful of napkins and got up and left McVie's. As he looked to the left before crossing College Street he noticed the light on in the Lutheran Campus Ministry.

Ω

Aaron had been adopted into a Jewish family. His father was descended from German Jews. His mother was of Russian and Polish ancestry. He had often wondered about the origin of the name Sullivan. Throughout his life Aaron had heard many versions of Opa Herschel's story, although none had come from Opa (Opa being the German form of grandpa). Highmen Sullivan's father had died from a sudden heart attack when Aaron was four years old. The story went that when Herschel and his family arrived at Ellis Island in 1923, they had been given a choice of names. The family name was Bragenstein. Aaron's Opa Herschel thought the Irish had a relatively strong reputation as the builders of New York. He thought combining the very Semitic Herschel with a ubiquitous Irish surname would confuse anyone intending to stereotype him. To further confuse those looking to stereotype him, Aaron's father changed the spelling of his first name from the traditional *Hyman*. So far his plan had worked and bullies had been stymied by Aaron's interchangeable adopted name. The biblical name Aaron preceding the patently Irish Sullivan provided the categorically challenged with scant opportunity for decisive reasoning. "What are you?" was what he heard all through grade school when placing people in a castigating category was the best recourse of the hormonally frustrated. When Aaron happened to divulge one day that he was Jewish, it was like he had signed a deal with Lucifer. From that day forward, his pre-pubescent nemeses were provided with ample ammunition to bring them through to high school. However, ammunition implies a defense. What was he defending? He was secure with himself. Try as he did, he could never find a logical need to care about what others were doing, why they were doing it and what the psychological implications might be. "You killed Christ," he often heard, oddly enough from those kids whose parents force-fed them Bible scripture. Even as a child, he knew that the Jews could not be held responsible for the demise and subsequent deification of Jesus.

To be fair, Jesus was not killed by Aaron or any one of the Jews throughout history, adopted or otherwise. Actually, had Jesus not met with his untimely death at the hands of whomever chose to denounce him, the entire premise of the Christian religion could not stand. It had been prophesied in the Bible. Its words, however, gave no explanation of when, how or at whose hands the deification happened. The Bible simply indicated that it would happen and the part of humanity that accepted it might prosper. So the way Aaron saw it, it was serendipity smiling in the face of irony. Why would the Jews kill one of their own? Highmen and Shirley were Jews who had taken in a son. Mary and Joseph had delineated their Jewish heritage to Jesus.

Ron had a way of concealing hostility that was likely a useful tool for marriage. He kept to himself, as if nothing had ever happened to upset Aaron.

"*You* don't think the Jews killed Christ?"

Ron looked sheepishly at his roomy and shrugged. Who could break the ice? Lord knows Aaron had tried. Ron was happy in his own world, although probably a little ashamed and embarrassed for insulting him. He lacked the courage to admit it though.

"Man, I know you think what you said over at McVie's upset me. I can get over it. Confront it, will you? God can't do it for you. You said it, you can't take it back. But *I* can get over it. You think I have my head in the clouds? What is that supposed to mean? Is putting my life in perspective a waste of my time? Things are best left unanswered? You don't have the courage to even ask the questions. I think you're scared. You're so afraid of getting the answer that you don't even ask the question." Ron stopped at the door and turned to face Aaron.

"You know, you think too much about life. I'm happy. I don't complicate things. I saw those pamphlets from the Lutheran Campus Ministry on your desk. Are you thinking of becoming a Lutheran now?"

"You're not that religious are you?"

Ron instantly walked to his desk and slid open a drawer. He extracted a shabby cream-colored pamphlet. "This is what I think of religion. I started this underground publication a few years ago with some friends from my hometown. It is called *The Minnesota Christ Watch.*"

The cover depicted an animated man, clearly self-conscious of His own presence, running from the shadow of one tree to another. His white robe flowed as he ran, his small sandals precariously holding onto his feet. He had a look of wonderment on his face. Aaron turned the page to find a list of "Christ sightings." One claimed He was seen in the ramparts at Fort Snelling. He was also said to have been spotted driving a late model Volvo near the Minnesota River bottoms. The funniest said He was seen at K-mart in the defective merchandise room being commanded to perform miracles. Aaron handed the pamphlet back to Ron.

"I gotta admit Ron, I find this blasphemous. It is totally disrespectful. You're mocking something thousands believe."

"Chill out man. Don't take it so seriously. I bet if you told the boys from the Lutheran Campus Ministry about it they might chuckle. Try to look at this way—it's like Elvis sightings. We all know deep down the guy's dead. Yet some irrational part of our psyche makes him alive. It allows us to have fun suggesting his presence in the least likely places," he explained passionately, leaving no question that this was what *he* believed.

"If they aren't offended by it at the ministry I bet it's because they know you will pay in the end."

"Come again?"

"I highly doubt they'd condone such blatant mockery. They would just pray for your ignorance. See, by their calculations you are next in line to be Satan's right hand man. In the end, old JC will come at His appointed time to make His judgment of you. He will say that you have genuinely mocked His existence, made glib references to His staff and sandals, and duly equip you with hoofs and a pitchfork," Aaron joyfully pontificated.

"Maybe, if I subscribed to all that hokum. I don't, obviously. You have quite an imagination. Look, I don't care if those God squaders look down their waxy noses at hell-bound wretches like me. I know they just can't handle life themselves so they've created an illusionary world and its commander-in-chief."

"Who's that?"

"JC," Ron sighed, rolling his eyes.

"You think He calls all the shots?"

"I *know* He calls all the shots. They are like little marionettes. He pulls all the strings to make them real boys. They don't take out the trash without consulting Him. It's truly pathetic. Even athletes won't take full credit for their accomplishments. I see Olympic gold medal winners thanking God. Who had the motivation and strength to excel at their sport? God, Jesus, some invisible kinetic force?"

"Well obviously the athletes ultimately are credited for their success. Didn't you ever think that believing in something higher and more powerful than yourself might actually be a need of some people?"

"Is it a need of yours?"

"I doubt it. At least at this point I can manage on my own. Although I think you are doing yourself a disservice by mocking Christ with cartoons like this. You might feel differently someday. Don't burn your bridges. It is also an insult to those who stake their life on the idea of a higher power." Aaron leaned back in his chair, resting on his laurels, satisfied that he had appeased the campus ministry by verbally crucifying his roommate.

"Thanks for the insight. Man, lighten up will you!" Ron shouted as he settled down at his desk, feigning deep thought with his nose in his only notebook.

"I'll bet you're one of those happy-go-lucky souls that never allows a metaphysical idea into his head."

"Maybe I am, but you'll never know."

"You got something to hide?"

"No, I just don't think most things life throws at me are worth examining," Ron scoffed, scratching his bald spot. He sucked on the red mustache that hung down over his mouth. This was a sign that he was suppressing something. Aaron always knew this but he never let on that he did. When it was appropriate, he cornered his roommate in hopes of seeing him squirm a bit. Ron never did though.

"Why, why do you want to know," he demanded. "You writing a research paper?"

"No, just asking. Man, don't get so defensive."

"Ok. You can hang with the Jesus freaks, you can go looking for bio-mom. Just don't ask me about it, tell me about it, or implicate me in any way. Deal?"

"Sure, no problem. Man, what a hot head."

"Don't push me Sullivan."

"Give it a rest Ron." Aaron calmly whispered as he grabbed his backpack and headed off to class.

Ω

"You know Jesus loves you."

"I'm not surprised. I'm a very likable person."

"Ross, Ross Bessinghalt," he said extending a tiny mittened hand. "I'm head of the campus ministry. I saw you looking around the other day. Searching for something?"

A short man stood staring at Aaron with a smile that looked involuntarily muscled. It either meant he was full of the Lord's words or that he was simply a person who didn't take anything too seriously. He had an unconvincing southern drawl. His horn-rimmed glasses rounded his little bowl-cut head with room to spare, giving him the appearance of a wise, but irritating owl. He, like many Christians Aaron had met, had a transparent charm through which one might plunge the dull end of a knife. He was condescending and arrogant but disguised those qualities with an insurmountable product to sell. Ross was just doing what anyone would do who had felt the sanguine sediments of Christ's sandals between their toes. However, when the Holy Grail is discovered, the condescension becomes forgivable. Aaron could not totally dismiss the worth of Christ to these people. Who was he to say that everything they had read and based their lives on was not true? Aaron had been raised to believe that Jesus, who happened to meet with destiny in Nazareth, was only a man. He preached something that was not widely embraced and he was killed for it in a manner that was common in the first century AD. End of story.

"Possibly," he shrugged. "Just weighing my options I guess."

"Nothing wrong with that my friend," Ross smiled, placing his hand on Aaron's shoulder. "But you do know God loves you and he sent his only Son to die for your sins," Ross instructed.

"You don't say? Say, how did you know I had sins?"

"Man is born with sin and then it is washed away when he is baptized."

"Well, I was raised Jewish. Never baptized. I'm circumcised though. Will that get me anywhere safer than a bed with a Shiksa (young non-Jewish woman)? See Ross, Jews are born destined to sin, it's a given. There is no absolution in our world. Only one day of atonement each new Jewish year, Yom Kippur."

"Are you satisfied with that?"

"Are you?"

"Frankly, no. We could do better. With Christ in your world you don't have to carry all that guilt around the whole year. Embrace Christ and soon sin will be non-existent. It will be the stuff of your prior existence. You will no longer be *in* the world, playing the game. You will be *of* it," Ross prattled on, never having quite released his hand from Aaron's shoulder. As Ross's credibility as a messenger of the Lord was put into question, the grip tightened. It was as if at any point Ross expected Aaron to leave him. Aaron pried Ross's mittened hands from his shoulder and smoothed them tidily at his side.

"Friend, do you believe in destiny?"

"Not really. Christ died so we would not have to worry about that. 'For God so loved the world–"

"Yeah yeah, I'm well acquainted with the quote. Could my destiny be to find my parents?"

"Oh my. Brother, are you an orphan?"

The condescending sound of Ross's voice returned.

"No. I was adopted when I was two weeks old. Something is compelling me to find at least one of my biological parents."

"Why, are you unhappy at home?"

"Oh no. I was adopted by a wonderful family. I just learned of my origin a few years ago."

"So for most of your life you never wondered about your roots?"

"I guess you might say that. I just never realized that my mom or dad looked nothing like me. Ross, I'm confused."

A beacon-like glimmer suddenly glazed over Ross's eyes as he sensed a soul yearning to be saved. There was no altruism in their world. Everything was connected to a higher purpose. Ross was a testament to that. Aaron was another notch on the staff with which Ross beat the sand out of his sandals each night. He was just another bread crumb lining the trail out of this world. Ross's eyes became a cistern for tears designed to corroborate his story.

"My friend, Jesus has been knocking on your door for most of your life. If you answer it, He might lead you to your destiny. He's the only one that knows what it is."

"He *might?* You mean he could leave a flaming bag of dog poo at my door? That's what I'm afraid of Ross. See, my way I am in control of things. If things don't work out, I can deal with it on my level. Your way, I'm tossing up my life to someone who *might* be out there taking notes on my life. Ross, why must you go around scaring poo out of people and their dogs, taking Jesus and pawning Him off on losers like me? What'd He ever do to you?"

"My friend, bear with me. It might seem like a long-shot at first, but still He loves you unconditionally," Ross pontificated.

"So finding my parents wouldn't be a mistake, it would work out for me, guaranteed?"

"Yes. And if it doesn't, it wasn't meant to be."

"What help is that? There is no guarantee of success, no promise of fulfillment."

"No, to be honest. But if it goes wrong Christ is at the helm now to pick up the pieces."

"Again with the hand on the shoulder? Is this where people usually tell you to get lost, when they find out you're nothing but a pitch-man with a faulty product? Ross, love is not a commodity. Compassion, understanding and a real trust in life can't be made into a commercial."

Ross threw his hands up and shook his little round face in confusion. "How so? I don't follow."

"Well," Aaron sighed as he watched Ross try desperately to get out of this world with as many fans as he could, "you're telling me that if I surrender my life to your man JC I can win either way. Basically it's a no-fault insurance plan." Ross still peered out at him as though Aaron was fading from sight. "Say I follow what I believe is my destiny, you know, to find my biological father or mother. The worst case scenario is that he or she slams the door in my face, proceeds to harass me, drives a wedge between me and my folks and finally I end up on some shrink's couch for the next ten years. The plan you're pitching provides that Christ will take care of all that. He will fix everything."

It appeared to Ross that his friend had come back and his smile returned like the sun from an eclipse.

"Of course He will, no question about it."

"Sorry chief, life is more complicated than that for me. I know it's a crap-shoot and I'm prepared to take it as it comes. No, I can't believe that anything in this world can put a guarantee on fate. That's the whole concept of fate, getting by on the utter uncertainty of it. Surviving, staying optimistic and motivated in spite of it. That's the real deal in life. There are no illusive shepherds, no ill-conceived insurance plans, just human calculations and the conviction to follow those educated guesses," Aaron carefully explained, noticing that their short walk had encompassed the campus. Ross looked at Aaron over the rim of his glasses squinting as though the condensation was impairing his sight. "Still, you may want to join us at our Bible study. We meet at 7 each Monday night. You know where we are, right next to McVies. Grab a slice and come on over. So, maybe I'll see you there. I will pray for you."

And there they were, the five most condescending words in the English language. These words had accosted Aaron's ears all too often. The assumption is made that the one who is prayed for requires the nurturing a clasp of hands and a sympathetic mind can provide for their life. What if they didn't need it? The praying is wasted. Aaron wondered if anyone had ever responded to that platitude with, "Thanks, I could sure use it." He had doubts.

Aaron watched Ross as he strode into the sinking twilight, his bony shoulders bouncing lightly as his little bowl-cut head bobbled in perfect cadence. He was perfect. Self-important, pompous, one could say. At least that was how he sold himself. Nothing was seen up front but smarmy, hollow charm. There was also a willingness to be the butt of jokes or object of flippancy many people might use to their advantage. His facial muscles must have been exhausted at the end of the day. Even so, Ross was only providing a way through this world to the next. Aaron could not hold that against him. He did insult people's intelligence along the way, but that is often written off as a casualty of soul-saving. God accordingly created human intellect and the various levels and quotients. He created it, so what's wrong with His agent degrading it some if it achieves a loftier purpose? Perhaps Ross and his merry band had taken a page from Machiavelli. They did hide their expediency with things like a poor affectation of a Southern drawl. Their deceit was usually obscured by glasses, a flamboyant hat or a hollow charm.

Ω

"So has your friend given you a training staff and sandals yet?"

"He's not really my friend Ron. I think he's got issues of his own. I like talking to the guy, okay. It gives me assurance that I'm doing the right thing."

"Oh, how's that work?"

"I haven't really figured it out yet. All I know is that he makes me more determined to keep believing in what I know."

"Funny how it works that way, you know," Ron mused as he hoisted himself to his bunk with a great huff that exceeded his age by several years. "Be careful what you wish for buddy, or who you listen to in this life. Man, look at me. I don't ask anything of anyone, I don't go poking around in the past and I'm a happy man," he sighed as he stretched out with his hands folded neatly behind his head on his pillow.

"And I'm not? I suppose you're happy because you're embezzling from your employer."

"No, no, it's not that at all," he shot back. "Look, if you're bothering those Bible-thumpers there's something wrong only you can fix. They've got enough problems, you know, carrying the sins of everyone on their shoulders and all. Those do-gooders must be awfully tired at the end of the day."

"Well, maybe that's why I'd like to help them, to ease their burden. You ever think of that hot-shot?"

"No, I just thought it was you being the metaphysical, debate-seeking junkie that you are. Sulli, you go looking for trouble. Trust me, don't get caught up with these rubber-neckers. They think they hold life's answers in the palms of their manicured little hands and they think they will die if they don't broadcast it to the world."

Aaron felt a deep pang of sympathy for his roommate. He sensed how Ron's distrust and subsequent apathy towards the world trapped him.

"You know, Ron, lately I've been leaning towards declaring my major in psychology," Aaron said in sarcasm's subtext. "I find it fascinating how people deal with life, why they do what they do. Or, in your case, why they don't deal with life."

"Jesus, here we go again," Ron sighed. "Okay, for a chuckle, tell me why I think all your searching for this and that is a huge waste of time."

"How should I know," he shrugged, "I haven't even taken any classes yet."

"You must have an idea."

"I think I mentioned it once before. You don't remember?"

"No, don't recall."

"I think that says it right there. The mere fact that you don't remember tells me that you're even apathetic toward the root of your apathy. You're, one might say, pathologically apathetic."

Ron's thinning red hair drooped, limply matting itself to a reddened face. He fidgeted on the edge of his bunk, his legs now dangling like two unbalanced pendulums. He abruptly sprang to the floor and began to feign study at his desk.

"I rest my case."

"Get lost."

"Hey, don't be sore at me just because you're a parasite."

"What are you babbling about now?"

"You know exactly what I mean. You play the role of the content little working stiff, busting his tight ass to get ahead. All the while you have a little scheme going with an attitude of 'who's the wiser.' Right?" Aaron nodded and waited patiently for Ron to follow his lead. "You live vicariously through people like me who actually examine why things are the way they are."

An unruly cow-lick discovered at Ron's infrequent glances in the mirror was left to have its way with his head. He chose his battles with all the tenacity of a puritan's apprentice. Aaron never expected Ron to retaliate completely, never in any way that might someday bring karma to his life. He was a crafty one though, flogging anyone who came in his path with apathy disguised as mockery towards their life and his. The result might be a kind of tenuous friendship, an acquaintance that never advances past small-talk.

The people in the dorm always asked Aaron about Ron. He might hear, "Your roommate's weird," or "How old is that guy? He looks like he's forty-eight." Aaron did not really talk about Ron much to anyone. Unlike other roommates who usually succeeded in achieving some kind of friendship by graduation, Ron and Aaron never got much further than watching *M*A*S*H* together and having the occasional slice of pizza.

Ω

November dumped snow on the tiny campus, curiously relenting only at the steps of the Lutheran Ministry. Aaron studied at his cube-like desk, occasionally glancing out the window to see the endless parade of students surrealistically sliding by in their Sorrel boots. He tried to focus on his studies but his mind drifted like the snow that piled up under the window. His mind had been plagued with the anticipation of receiving a letter from his biological mother. Ron was of no help. He swiftly answered every opportunity to make his feelings clear that inquiries such as Aaron's were futile and fraught with potential disasters. When he had finally abandoned trying to focus on his English essay about his trip to East Berlin, he heard a jingling at the door.

"Sulli," Ron nodded and threw a few pieces of mail on Aaron's desk.

"How was class this morning?"

"You missed a classic Rublitzky moment. He lectured on the empiricism of the Easter rabbit, all the while looking like a bloated rabbit himself."

"Did you take notes?"

"You know me, I keep it all in my head. He lectured on the theories of philosophers like David Hume and John Locke. Did you ever believe in the Easter rabbit?"

"What do you think? I'm Jewish."

"Okay, did you ever believe the Red Sea parted so all those staffs and sandals could run through it?"

"Hardly a fair comparison now, isn't it."

"Old man Rublitzky said that all knowledge is a product of sense-experience. Let's say in a Gentile household the kid is taken to see some putz in a rabbit suit every Easter until he becomes wise enough to realize that there are no man-sized rabbits. Or, in the Jewish house, every year a kid hears the story of the Exodus from Egypt crossing the Red sea on foot. Sense-experience," Ron smiled haughtily.

"Have you ever believed in either?"

"God no—I'm not that gullible!"

"So, in the case of the Passover story, believing something written in the bible is being gullible?"

"Depends who you ask. I'll bet there's a twenty-one year old somewhere who still thinks life-size rabbits lay eggs behind bushes each year, and they're probably in the nut hutch."

"Ron, there are wise rabbis, educated Orthodox-Jewish men who believe everything happened exactly the way it's written in the Book of

Exodus from the Torah. Are you going to recommend they be put away with the bunny believers?"

General psychology was the only class the roommates took together. Most of Ron's classes took place on the other side of campus. Everet G. Rublitzky was the professor of psychology. He had an unkempt crop of gray hair that served well to distract people from his round wire-rimmed glasses. He wore the same stained gray trousers and yellow sweater for weeks at a time. Aaron got the impression that college professors must not be paid very well. He wondered where all the tuition he was paying was going. Dr. Rublitzky, as he insisted on being called (even though research had revealed to Aaron that Everet was not a PhD), always came to class with at least a three o'clock shadow to hide the unnatural cragginess of his face. He was amusing to watch and Ron and Aaron delighted in watching his animated movements around the room.

"Say Sulli, who is Jane Swenson?"

"How do you know that name?"

"This letter I forgot to give you from yesterday has her return address."

"Give me that!"

"Say please," Ron said as he waved it in the air.

"Give it to me. It's from my biological mother."

"Ohhh, the bio-mom. Well then, this is a big day for you."

"Can the dramatics and give me my letter."

"Are you going to share it with your Christian buddy?"

"Probably not. If I do, why would I tell you?"

He snatched his letter and opened it. Aaron cleared his desk and spread the letter on the white surface, sterile under the bright florescent desk light. Now he could focus on one thing. He shifted his thoughts about having gone through mazes and checkpoints to get to the gray, policed streets of East Berlin to falling into the warm embrace of the woman who put him in this world.

Like the Virgin Mary, Jane had found herself with impending

motherhood. Fate had selected Aaron to be the baby Highmen and Shirley Sullivan raised. Jesus was born to a single-mother and divine intervention had placed him for adoption; Joseph had assumed the role of adoptive father. Just as fate arranged for Aaron, Jesus only knew his biological mother.

Shirley loved Aaron as her only son. For twenty years he had loved her as his only mother. Part of him felt guilty for *needing* to meet this woman who had given birth to him. The other part he had confided to Ross in hopes of guidance. Aaron was mesmerized by the letter from Jane. He stared at it, embedding the longings of his soul into each word. She wrote in the present, as if no time had ever elapsed.

"Ron, fate is like a road map. You can usually follow it right down the line, see why things happened the way they did."

"You really over-analyze things, you know. What if you finally meet this woman and you have nothing in common? What if she drives a permanent wedge between you and your ma? Aaron, you really don't know what you're doing here. You can't imagine the Pandora's box you're opening."

Ω

Snow had collected in vast quantities on the steps of the Commons at BSU, a disparaging indication that winter had no inclination of leaving for the next four months. A man appeared to Aaron, identifying him and following his tracks in the fresh snow. The hat, scarf, and thick winter coat made his utterance all the more prophetic. Aaron stood widening his tracks as his boots began to quake.

"God loves you."

"I thought it was Jesus. God too, huh?"

Aaron sensed a smile animating itself again beneath the scarf. His flippancy was innate, a product of feigned indifference perhaps. The man beneath the scarf scanned him cautiously as his eyes danced and his breath emanated from the scarf. Aaron wondered if this meant a new pope had been appointed to insult his intelligence.

"Aaron my brother, it's me. Remember—Ross Bessinghalt," a friendly voice erupted as a tiny hand magically reached up to pull the scarf down.

"Of course, how could I forget you? You're like my guardian angel."

"What was that?"

"I said guardian angel. I find it more than a coincidence that you came along when I was dealing with all this."

"Ah," Ross closed his eyes as a swath of fresh air cast a noose over him. "So you believe that someone out there is intending to guide you."

"Not totally. I still think you are up to something. I think you know deep in your heart that there is nothing really out there at all. It is your job to place figments, filaments if you will, in the flickering light bulb of the common sinner's mind." Ross's eyes turned hostile, enraged, sensing the over- exposure of his grifted presentation.

"If that metaphor works for you. Please Aaron, my brother, I am on the level. God is abundantly real, omnipresent, and omniscient too. Please believe me." He pleaded like a passive-aggressive carnival barker who urges people to throw rings at bottles. It was their job to make the participant's eyes create the illusion that the rings were wider than the bottles' necks.

"Stop calling me brother. You're not black and I highly doubt you're my biological brother. Not unless some genetic anomaly in my lineage provided DNA for round-faced, astigmatic simpletons who smile like elves are pinching the corners of their mouth!"

"Calm down. I certainly didn't mean to offend or upset you."

"Well you did."

Ross began to stroke the tassel on his hat continuously, causing it to bounce lightly as he spoke. The apparition was diabolical. Aaron was mesmerized as the tassel's gyrations provided the only proximal movement in the frigid November air. Ross obviously had the charisma of an evangelist with the shrewdness for flim-flam, a perfect melding for Aaron's vulnerability.

"Sorry for flying off the handle like that. God knows what I'd have been if I wasn't adopted by the Sullivans. They were all Orthodox Jews many generations ago. As I'm told, each generation was a bit more Reform. As Jewish law goes I'm not even a Jew. Unless my mother was a Jew, I'm not in the club. I think that's why I still need to know what's out there. I need to know what makes Gentiles like you think you have a monopoly on fate."

"The fact that Christ died for your sins." Ross slid effortlessly off his tongue. Although the sudden glare he gave Aaron begged for belief. "Sullivan, huh. That name must have a fascinating story behind it." He paused to scratch his chin, deep in thought. At first meeting him Aaron had truly expected Ross never to ask questions about his homogenized name. "It occurs to me now that Sullivan is usually Irish. Does your adopted family have any Irish heritage?"

"No, but the records I got at the adoption agency list my biological mother as having Irish ancestry."

"And what was her family name?"

"Swenson. Half Irish and half Swedish.

Ross raised his head in the air, craning his neck under the weight of his garments. He sighed heavily as though he was trying to hide himself from his next question.

"So—how did the Sullivans get their name? Please, tell me. Though if it makes you uneasy, I'd understand." He clasped Aaron's gloved hand.

"No, no, I don't mind," Aaron said, gazing at the barren branches scratching the frozen clouds against a chartreuse sunset. "The family name was, and still is legally, Bragenstein. My Opa Herschel came to this country from Celle, Germany in 1923. He and his family arrived at Ellis Island and settled in Throggs Neck in the Bronx. Throggs Neck was founded in 1624 by the Dutch. However the name comes from an Englishman named John Throckmorton who the Dutch allowed in their tiny peninsula formerly known as Vriedelandt." Aaron spoke thoughtfully, adding extra information he hoped would distract Ross from his original question.

"Boy, you sure know your history," Ross exclaimed, impressed with Aaron's factual logistics, "but you still haven't told me how Herschel Sullivan came to be."

"All right," he sighed. "You see at that time in New York, Jews were still excluded from a lot of places. Opa had this crazy idea that if he adopted a very Irish surname and kept his very Jewish first name people would be confused. They had no viable reason to assume he was Jewish. Well, fully Jewish anyway."

"Why Irish?"

"The story goes that Opa Herschel thought the Irish had a good standing in New York at the time," he shrugged. "Well, compared to the Jews anyways."

"So, did it work for him and his family?" Ross pressed, his wide eyes beaming behind foggy lenses.

"As far as I know it did. At least I remember him telling me when I was four that he thought the name had gained him access to more places than Bragenstein would have."

"How has it worked for you? I mean does anyone ever figure out that you're Jewish?"

"What do you think? I'm adopted for God's sake. I guess I do have some Semitic features though, now that I think about it. Once I spent a few weeks in Tel Aviv. They all thought I was Arab because of my dark complexion. When they asked my name and I said Sullivan they looked at me strangely like I had broken the Dead Sea scrolls or something. The officials knew my ethnicity though because my passport lists my name as Bragenstein. At least that adds up for them. You know, people need things to add up or they're not happy."

Ross nodded complacently.

The two estranged apostles began walking, skimming their feet along the shoveled parts of the Commons. As they approached the campus ministry, Ross stopped, wiped his glasses clear and carefully replaced them.

"You know Jesus was a Jew."

"Yes, I think I read that somewhere. Why are you telling me this now?"

Ross looked at Aaron as though he had painted the Sistine Chapel with a vulgar graffito. However, his eyes sluggishly schlepped along the indication that any graffiti might have been condoned by the pope.

"I tell you this now because you seem to be at a crossroads. You can go down one path and maybe find your destiny—maybe. The other path is much less ambiguous, much less likely to disappoint. Now, Jesus was a Jew and so were you. He strayed, he was the one true Christian," Ross spoke emphatically as the tears of a crocodile mingled with the condensation on his glasses.

"Yeah, and we all know how that worked out for him. Look Ross, I don't want to be crucified for what I do or don't believe. I know what I know and I'd like to hear what you know. I'm not saying I'll embrace it like you have or start passing out bibles on street corners." Aaron looked down College Street and was tempted to abandon Ross right there. As he walked away, he turned and studied Ross's face for any signs of defeat. Unaffected by Aaron's petulant departure, Ross unwrapped his scarf and he went inside the ministry.

"Wait a minute Ross."

"Yes," he turned in breathless anticipation.

"You consider what we have as a casual friendship, right?"

"Yes, I guess. Why do you ask?"

"Well, I want to know. I need to know right now whether your casual friendship hinges on my becoming a Christian." Ross turned around into the lasso of his scarf. He gazed into the heavens and shook his tiny, mittened fists. The game was over for him.

"No, to be honest I would not be your friend." He smiled and allowed the wind to tousle his hair. Christ had instantly forgiven him. Aaron had him on a technicality. Ross's faith dictated he had to be honest when push came to shove. Aaron was disappointed and disillusioned. He really expected more from one who threw around Christian theology with such passion. Ross had graciously drawn a line at his request. He had been forthright with Aaron, stamping on human emotion and expecting God to still give him a commission.

"Lost another one, eh Ross? Mark it in your ledger. I know you have one. Thanks for being honest though. Nice knowing ya."

He raised his arm and College Street parted to liberate Aaron from Ross. As quickly and as incidentally as he had come into Aaron's life, Ross was gone. He glanced across the street and saw Ross peering out the window, surely waiting for the next wandering Jew with a taste for pizza.

Ω

The melancholy moroseness of "Suicide is Painless," the theme song for *M*A*S*H*, balmed Aaron's blistered sense of himself. Its winsome melody allowed a pang of sympathy for Ross. How pathetic, how hypocritical was a man who professed to be doing the Lord's work when he was actually looking out for himself. How could Ross have pretended to be a friend for his own gain? Aaron fumbled with his keys and thought of the next patsy Ross tried to sell a ticket to immortality.

"Hey Ron. *M*A*S*H* just starting?"

"Sure is. How'd it go with the ministry of tom-foolery?"

"Guy turned out to be a real phony. I put the question right to him. I asked whether he'd be my friend if I never became a Christian. He politely responded in the negative."

"I could have saved you a few laps in the sandals my friend," Ron laughed. "So, did you learn anything for your humiliation?"

"Not really. Just that people are really out for themselves. There's always a motive. They wrap their sincerity in a righteous package called organized religion and sell it to desperate unholy, souls who pass by street corners."

"So you're admitting that you're a desperate, unholy soul?"

"I must have been when I met Ross."

"You aren't now? Who's to say you won't latch on to the next disciple of deception?"

"I can't say, Ron," Aaron sighed, humbly, hanging his head. "The best I can hope for is that I find the courage to find destiny on my own."

The two sat and watched their program quietly for several moments. Ron suddenly rolled his chair over to his desk and began scribbling something in a notebook. "Here. This is a statement of your intent, documentation of your being burned by the Christian, November 12, 1985."

"Don't worry, I won't forget."

"No, but if you do I will have this to remind you. I think it's time for McVie's.

Ω

"What's up for Thanksgiving, Aaron?"

His next door dorm neighbor was doing his dance in the hall. Clarence was portly and amusing to watch. It always seemed like a hat for money, placed cleverly at his feet, was appropriate.

"I'm flying out to Portland to see my mother."

"How long has it been?"

"This is our first meeting."

"Okay—and you were what, born in a Petri dish?"

"No, no, Lump," Aaron laughed, "I was adopted. I had an agency locate my biological mother about a month ago. She lives in Portland, Maine, with her cats and two daughters."

"And the cats would be your sisters?"

"Funny, but no. My mother was never married to my father. It sounds like he left about the time he found out I was on the way."

"Deadbeat, right? Couldn't deal with it."

"Well, I guess. See, I think the guy had a lot on his shoulders. He was all-American some school down South."

"Do you know his name?"

"No. All I know is that he went to a school in the South. I know he had African ancestry, which explains my dark complexion."

"Well that's news to me. I would have never guessed you had any black in you," Lumpy stepped back as a wry smile drew on his face. He began his dance again, designed to distract Aaron.

Clarence Dondercranz had invented the bizarre, salaciously animated character The Kamikaze Bologna. The brief dance consisted of a halting two-step cadence while wild gyrations brought Clarence's arms to surreal heights. Portly, stocky, merely teasing a wiry tuft of hair with an afro-comb each morning, Clarence had earned the moniker Lumpy not so much for his shape. The appellation derived from his sedentary lifestyle, a fact that made his ability to do this dance all the more amazing. He and Aaron stood under florescent dormitory light, Lump's arms flailing madly and feet kicking out to a rhythm tapped out from his omnipresent Walkman. He slowed to a stop.

"You must have something else in you then?"

"Well, my other is half Irish and half Swedish."

"Quite an eclectic mix you got there. Bet people scratch their heads a lot when ethnicity's a topic."

"Yes. I'm not sure why, but where my ancestors came from is usually a question I'm asked. It just invites stereotypes. I think on the average, people expect certain races and ethnicity to match stereotypes lodged in their brains. They are visibly uncomfortable. When I meet someone, their ethnicity is not a first curiosity of mine. If it comes up in conversation great, but really I couldn't care less." Lump listened to Aaron prattle on as he shook the last remnants from the Kamikaze Bologna.

"People see me and the shape of my head, my eyes, my kind of tapering nose and appear to be mentally running through a list of possible persuasions. I thought you were Mexican. The blue eyes though, that kind of confused that theory."

Clarence was no idiot. He was slovenly to say the least, but he always made his efforts work out in the end. He studied. He pulled good grades, or so everyone thought. He was still here, in his fifth year at BSU; he must have been doing something right. Lump was the most unlikely psychology student anyone had ever seen. He was lazy, frequently introverted and usually lacked any genuine concern about anyone's condition but his own and apparently not much for that even. He had spent years here, thousands of dollars, bleary eyed nights pouring over texts that rested in plastic sleds. He had smoked bags of pot, which he rarely shared and vomited in a full run down Main Street. Why he was still here no one knew.

"That's what I get the most of, people waiting for me to speak to them in Spanish. It's funny, you know. Most white folks have no idea where my ancestors came from while blacks know right away that I share some genetics with them. My freshman year here I got in with a group of blacks. They were mild activists and tried to shape racial attitudes on campus. It did not last. I just didn't fit. My suspicion is that I wasn't black enough."

Lumpy's reddened green oval eyes drifted off down the hall. He fixated on the covert antics of a forensics student bringing a skinned, embalmed cat into his room. The cat passed through the door with its tail hanging off the slab. No one knew much about this student who had been at BSU a short time. He was very studious, kind of a loner.

"Hey Clarence, what do you know about that guy?"

Lumpy studied Aaron thoroughly and then sighed like he had found something more familiar. No one at BSU had called him Clarence since his freshman year.

"Not much. I know he transferred here from some school down South. We hardly ever see him. The few times we do, he's always been up to something. We try to get him to hang out with us. I get the feeling he thinks a lot of himself," Lump said, pressing his nose upward. "Why are you so curious?"

"It's weird. He looks familiar, don't you think?" Aaron said, looking down the hall.

"Maybe a little, the dark complexion. Though that might just be because I've only seen him at dusk and the halls kind of throw a darker hue on some people." He quickly shuffled his feet to mime the dance he had invented, failing to regain Aaron's attention.

"Man, that's strange. It's like I've seen him somewhere before. I just can't remember when or where. Wouldn't that drive you crazy Lump?" Lumpy was now pumping his arms furiously in crude mechanics of the dance, all in an effort to distract Aaron. The cat's pink tail didn't move.

"Aaron my man, when is your plane leaving?" Lumpy paused, distracted by the cat that had filled their hallway with a nose-stinging ether smell, like a hospital that hadn't paid its electric bills and had begun to marinate in its medicinal properties.

"Friday morning. What are you doing for the holidays?"

"Nothing special. You know, just hold the fort down here. Someone has to, right?" Lumpy spoke with his hands, poking gingerly at the frosty windows as he practiced his smile.

"You have a family, don't you?"

"Yes. We're really not that close though," he said hanging his head in a mock effort to elicit sympathy from Aaron.

"You see them at Thanksgiving at least?"

"Well, every few years maybe," he laughed. "Ahh, family, who needs them."

"You miss the support of a family, don't you? Just a little?"

"Not really. I'm happy right here. Watching what the cat man does, doing the dance of death once in a while, getting high once in a while," he shook his fat, clenched fingers as he pleaded his case to Aaron.

"Okay then Lump, if you say so. I'll see you in a week then. Have a good Thanksgiving."

The two parted company. Lumpy immediately disappeared into his room which always worked out to be the closest exit. Aaron passed the forensics student's room on the way to his own. The door was ajar and he saw what floated in formaldehyde. A double-stranded helix apparition formed its silhouette as he passed the door.

Ω

A sufficient arsenal of snow elicited students' frustration. It absorbed any guilt that was produced by their suicidal ideations. The students' goal each week was to get through to the following Thursday evening.

"Got a ride to the airport Sulli?"

"Actually I was hoping I could bum a ride with you to the cities."

"Sure. I forget, where do you live?"

"Garrison. You know that."

"Your ma picking you up then?"

"Yeah, she'll be there.

Ron never told anyone where he lived. Aaron called Shirley that night and arranged a rendezvous at a little diner in Aitkin.

Thursday arrived overcome by anticipation. Concentration on academics was impossible. The mold his brain had been set in for the last three months had cracked, spilling out all the neurons formerly employed at BSU. His bag was packed along with his bulbous, green laundry bag. The day could not be expedited; every minute had to have its purpose. Aaron peered out the window of his classroom at Ron's Buick and pictured them speeding south. It was torture.

"So Sulli, set to go?"

"You know it. Got everything here."

"Great. Let's head out then"

Ron grabbed a grocery bag from the upper bunk. This was the only thing he ever took home. He always left his little portable TV, although when Aaron left he placed it even further back in his closet. His sleeping bag remained spread neatly on his bed, the only evidence that anyone else occupied the room.

"Five o'clock now. When did you tell your ma you'd meet her?"

"About six thirty. Will that work?'

"That's about right. A little over an hour."

The car doors slammed and Aaron was finally relieved of anticipation. He was on his way. Oddly enough, he was never anxious about actually meeting his bio-mom. He was anxious only about physically getting there. He had prescience about her accepting him with open arms.

Ron deposited Aaron at the diner along Aitkin's frontage road. "Well, good luck. Hope it's worth all your effort."

"I really didn't do that much."

"Didn't you have to pay some fee for the search?"

"Yeah, but that is really insignificant. I mean, to me anyway, this is a big deal. I know you make light of it and wouldn't invest a dime in finding your biological parent."

"No, I wouldn't," he looked at Aaron, making him feel like he was Jack in that beanstalk story who squandered his money on beans. "What'd it cost you?"

"Oh, I don't remember. It's really not important. You can't put a price on reality."

"Have a good one Sulli." He waved and sped away.

"Hi Mom."

"How are you Aaron? All set for this?"

"Sure, I guess so," he shrugged. "Unless you or Dad have a problem with it? I'd call it off if you did, even now," Aaron said, remembering Ross's glib affections. "I mean it. If this will upset you I don't have to do it. My relationship with you is most important."

"Aaron, didn't we go over this? Your concern for our feelings is very thoughtful. I know how much this means to you though."

"All right. As long as you're fine with it."

"I am. I can't say for your father. You know we don't talk that much. How often do you communicate with your father?"

"Not that often. I thought something this big would supersede any separation animosities."

"No, I'm sorry. It doesn't."

They sped on in an awkward silence until the city limits of Onamia were in their sights. The streets were slick with a day of rain on them as streetlights bounced their red or green hypnotic glance. Stop or go? Fate was toying with Aaron. He mused on what Ross might say. He could hear Ron giving flippant advice. Aaron thought of Lumpy dancing around like a fool in the dorm. He did not have to worry about finding a parent, dealing with a family—or losing a family.

Aaron was never close with his father. Since his parents' separation three years ago, they had hardly spoken at all. He had grown up in the atmosphere of a loveless marriage as an only child. He had no one to share the pain of seeing his parents ride out the hard times, if only for his sake. Aaron always wondered whether his mom was able to bear a child. Perhaps they just didn't love each other enough to create one. Either way, they had given Aaron a happy home for twenty years.

Ω

"Flight seven eighty-four to Portland now boarding …" alerted Aaron. He quickly gathered up his few carry-on items and settled in line.

"Where are you traveling today, sir?"

"Uh, oh, are you talking to me?"

"Of course I am silly."

A young woman stood holding a caged cat. The cat looked as though it expected euthanasia at any moment. However its whiskers conveyed confidence, as though the cat knew it had at least seven more lives.

"Sir? How old do you think I am?" The young woman looked slightly embarrassed, while her cat now paced in its cage in frustration. The woman could not have been much more than eighteen. Her jet black hair parted sharply at the side tracing a meandering trail to eyes as blue as Windex. For her age, she had quite a figure, an upper-body development which exceeded that of the college co-eds Aaron knew. Not a trace of modesty hid her body. She displayed her cleavage to Aaron and the entire airport as she bent to assist her cat.

"My Schadenfreude looks so sad. Oh, how old–I don't know. Thirty I'd guess."

"I'll be twenty-one in a few months. My name is Aaron," he said extending his hand hoping she'd shake it after tending to her cat.

"I'll take my foot out of my mouth now," she smiled meekly. Now he knew how Ron must feel all the time.

"My name's Sabina. I'm going to Portland to see some friends. From there I go home to Lubeck, Germany."

"You don't have any trace of a German accent."

"It's a compelling story. One I might tell someone's kids someday," she added with a grimace.

"Yours?"

"Maybe. Gotta find the right man first though. How 'bout you? You visiting family in Portland?"

"Sort of."

"What do you mean? You either are or you are not," she demanded.

"It is my biological mother. I'm meeting her for the first time." Sabina furrowed her black, bushy brow. Her lower lip protruded in a mock pout.

"Oh, you are so brave. I located my biological mother a few months ago. It didn't go well at all."

"So, you're adopted. It's ironic, me meeting you now. Tell me, how did it go so bad?"

Sabina poked a delicate finger through the cage to bristle the cat between the ears. Its eyes grew narrow with a tranquility which indicated that the suicidal thoughts had begun to subside. Schadenfreude had apparently decided to tough out the second life it had begun. Sabina sighed in frustration's spite. She held her head up and straight bangs fell against a pale face.

"I really would prefer not to talk about it. Let's just say we were not compatible. I do hope things work out for you though," she said with an unexpected smile.

"Are you together?"

"Uh—yes," they nodded in awkward synchronicity.

"You would like to sit together?"

"Sure, if no one takes the seat."

Ω

A line of crimson sun cut through the flowers of a bedspread's design. Sabina rubbed sleep from her eyes. Schadenfreude was coiled secure in her cage. Aaron's courage had gained momentum only to succumb to gravity as soon as his plane left the ground. His liaison with Sabina might have influenced his decision to meet Jane. He wondered whether Sabina genuinely empathized with him. He had vowed to himself that he would meet his mother on his own terms. Jane Swenson was ten years younger than Shirley. She was from a generation who put much less emphasis on connections. She had aspired to the hippie generation, a band of rebels who had created a counter-culture that lived life by the seat of its faded dungarees. If Jane had been Aaron's mother, the connection with Ron in Aitkin would not have happened. His life would have most likely panned out with much fewer situations where logistical accuracy was required and

Aaron himself would be able to feel the ambiguous threads in the worn seat of his jeans as they flew.

"Guten morgen, Aaron. Hast du gut geschlafen?"

"Ja, danke."

"You understand me? Where did you learn German?"

"Took three years in high school," he yawned. "Und du?"

"Von meinem Eltern, naturlich."

"From your parents? Sehr gut.

"You named your cat Schadenfreude? What exactly does that mean?"

"Oh it's an old German expression meaning finding joy in someone else's misfortune," she explained, winking seductively. "Why, do you think it's relevant to our situation now?" She had started to run her fingers down Aaron's chest, stopping just as she approached the bed covers. She sat naked on the edge of the bed, void of the subtle inhibitions inbred in most American women. Her eyes blinked twice to extract the last remnants of sleep. She lay back across the foot of the bed, stretching her body like a witch on a confession rack.

The flight had been long. Both craved sleep before facing their respective obligations. They had rented a car, gotten a room and gone to sleep. However, it was a totally chaste sleep, not the kind of sleep in which the words *sleep* and *together* progressively mesh to simultaneously arrive at sex. The sunrise streamed through the curtain's opening irritating Aaron's less honorable musings of Sabina. Was it possible that this woman was related to him through adoption? Celle was in a familiar vicinity of Lubeck. If that were the case, Aaron rationalized, any feelings he had still were permissible. Even so, the light insidiously illuminated parts of Sabina he knew he shouldn't see or enjoy seeing. A vengeful sun bled a stream of temptation from the dense black hairs covering her pubic region to blind him.

"Why did you stop there?"

"Did you want me to go farther down?"

"Not really, just curious I guess. You would though, wouldn't you?"

"Perhaps," she sat smiling sweetly. "Aaron, we're just friends, casual acquaintances who happened to end up in a motel room together."

Aaron closed his eyes and tried to remove any sexual thoughts from his conscious that had begun to rise. He studied Sabina's body the way he thought the forensics student might.

"Es freut mich sie kennen zu lernen."

"You're glad to get to know me? That's a bit formal for now, seeing that we just spent the night together."

"Es tut mir lied … I'm sorry. It's the first polite German phrase I learned."

"Literally it means it brings you joy to know me," she said, teasing Aaron with her feminine wiles.

"I know. Please stop doing that."

"Was ist los? Does my nakedness offend you?"

"No. What you do with it does. Sabina, who do you live with now? I mean what is your relationship with the parents that adopted you?"

"Please Aaron, it's too early to discuss such things. I mean really, who cares? I'm eighteen and looking for a place of my own. I don't care if no one wants me, loves me or cares whether I live or die. I'll just keep going until I find the right man," she grimaced as she flicked a piece of lint from her hair. No modesty, no inhibition. Reckless abandon with a cat in tow. She got up and liberated Schadenfreude from her cage. Sabina was a bit ditsy, too eccentric possibly, for Aaron's tastes. Had he been raised by his biological mother he might have seen her differently.

"I'm not then I guess?"

"Why, do you want to be?"

"Maybe," he said slowly as he peeled back the covers. She looked away, masking embarrassment. Aaron looked quizzically at her.

"It's okay for you to brazenly exhibit your body to me, but mine somehow offends you?"

"No, it's not that at all. You just startled me." She smiled demurely at Aaron, quickly freeing herself from the bed, the inquisitors having found her guilty. She hung her head in shame. She began to dress, leaving him naked and confused.

Ω

"That was awkward."

"Yeah, it was, wasn't it. I wish you luck meeting your mother."

"So this is it, huh?"

She nodded hesitantly, "Will I see you again?"

Sabina produced a crumpled scrap of paper from her tightly worn blue jeans. She squeezed it hard into Aaron's trembling hand. She kissed him intently on the cheek and picked up her cat. A rusty framed backpack was covered with patches from hostels of the world. Aaron helped her hoist it to her back. She kissed him again and hiked off with Schadenfreude.

He opened the paper as the fellow motor lodgers packed their SUVs. *SABINA HOFFERMEIER; CALL ME–281-439-6851. HOPE YOU FIND THE RIGHT WOMAN.* The tiny motor lodge stationary fluttered in the wind and he wondered if the number on the paper was even valid. Sabina was the type of scatter-brain that gave bogus numbers to people, on purpose or even by mistake. Apparently any intimacy Aaron thought existed after seeing each other naked had not penetrated her wall of black bangs. She'd left without telling him anything about her parents which led him to wonder whether she even had parents. He tossed the paper into the exhaust stream of an idling SUV and watched the pastel pink and blue colored stationary ripen in the heat. He quickly packed his suitcase, paid their bill and set out to find the euphoric feeling he once had. The one Mari Whiting had conveyed to him over the phone. The one he had when he first read Jane's letter. The one Ron, Ross, Clarence and Sabina had stolen from him.

The Divining Weeks

As the disciple of a born-again Christian, I wore my resolves on my sleeves. Religion, with all its enlightening commands and promises, was displayed to me like a smorgasbord. I'd become a seeker of truth–real truth, not the one according to say, Job. Prayers are rarely answered in college. There is usually too much on the mind to really be convincing. I didn't necessarily want one fulfilled, although the source of such sorcery intrigued me. I wanted to know if there was an inherent direction in life, my life to be exact. I would have settled for the conjured paths on which religion could guide me. I also wanted to find out why some Christians give off that elusive, inadvertent vibe that you are on the wrong road while they are merely on earth to save the day. It probably was that this phantom feeling was in my head just waiting to be awakened someday. If that was the case, it was truly diabolical, although it may very well have been just me projecting my feelings of doubt and inadequacy on them because I was sure that born-again Christians, if anyone, would know where I'm headed. They bear the cross of informational power.

I was curious about how Christianity worked. An authority on the subject happened to be a door knock away. I begged my dorm mate to fill me in on the magic he had once found. Not necessarily to join the club, surrender my soul or invest my squandered life in a sound insurance plan, but just to hear what was available. He worked on me. Figuring he had found a venerable soul with sympathy for anything that would answer some questions, my dorm mate set about loosening my already tenuous hold on my life. I had been raised a Jew in the Reform practice and as far as I knew, Jesus Christ was just a man who put his sandals on one foot at a time to slide across the water. He taught an amalgamation of the religion that the Roman Empire practiced. For this he was crucified and left to die what is described to have been a heinous and subsequently exploited death. I'd grown up thinking there is no reason for a Jew to believe in Jesus in the spiritual sense. To do so would, as I understood, contradict everything Judaism, a religion over 3,000 years older, taught.

We'd discuss religion, philosophy, life and occasionally college, in his room, often late into the night. I guess he wanted the home field advantage because proselytizing works best in a room whose walls had been tendered with nightly prayers. My room was the springboard from which miraculous transformations would flourish. I may have seen—or thought I saw—a bible or a French fry scuttle across the floor. My dorm door had a frosted transom above it. One night it was open a crack as I was studying. I turned my head in time to see a bible slip through the crack and lightly smack the tile floor. I was familiar enough with the laws of physics to know that the book could not have risen up to the window by its own power. My suspicion was that my dorm mate climbed on something and slid it through as though the opening were a mailbox. Even so, there should have been a noise like a gentle brushing at my door. Maybe I was so engrossed in my study of physical geography that I didn't hear it. Still, at other times, even at odd hours of the evening, I'd hear a slow, hollow knocking on my door. I chose to ignore all these phenomena knowing that my dorm mate and his other Christian friends in the dorm were fond of playing practical jokes. But in the back of my mind a question festered, a question to which I may have known the answer: Could God be working through these people to create these illusions?

The power of suggestion avails itself only to those with some moral incentive. It offers itself up like a seductress to the spiritually vulnerable. Then faith follows humbly with its contrite message that you can do better and your life is worth less without it. The messages, like that of my dorm mate, were all the same though. They weren't anything I couldn't have found in the depths of a beer mug or from the street-corner prophets. They all crooned the same to me, whether they were those proselytizing on the mall downtown or the mercenaries in the gym. They braised my eyes as I left them to consider following the paths they so conveniently and sanctimoniously offered me. Eventually, as tears filled their eyes, they told me that I can't live without this gift they had received. They had handed their worthless lives to Jesus and now begged me to do the same. They told me through derision and sublimation that I was at a crossroads and the window of opportunity was quickly drawing shut. On all accounts, the implication was clear to me: I should take the right path, the one they had laid out for me. But the choice was mine. If I walked away, I was still under their wing. We might even remain friends, although a part of them would always look down on me.

It was a no-win testimonial. Both sides needed to be happy, satisfied, sanctified and redeemed. That's a lot to ask from within the walls of a dorm room where most impetuously conceived deals with a higher power are made. For such saplings to be rooted requires an expanded mind, one free of contradicting thoughts from a Reform Jewish background.

In the midst of the various inter-campus groups was one called "Jews for Jesus." It sat at the end of the commons at a table off the path. The Baptists and even the New Agers had more recruits. There was even a group whose philosophy amounted to glorified fascism that aroused curiosity. And then, at the end of the hall, like a reprieve from all the other mind games, sat the Jews for Jesus. They claimed that I was half-way there and that I might as well complete the journey. I assumed "there" meant God and/or Jesus and the tranquility that came from accepting either into your heart. Their logic was simple; Jesus was a Jew and had led his disciples into his faith. One problem: I knew that Judaism pre-dated His teachings by more than 3,000 years. I thought the whole idea of Jews embracing

Jesus was anathematizing. It was sad and did its best to hide a self-righteous ignorance for what Judaism really is–or was.

Still my friend–a true friend regardless of my acceptance of his faith–worked on me. He consented to go with me to hear Jesse Jackson speak on campus. As a reciprocal gesture, I went with him to hear his presidential candidate that year–Pat Robertson. And then one spring night in 1988, my faculties relented. I was worn out and my life was in a tailspin of excessive drink, weekly house parties and the daunting challenge to graduate from college. My friend indulged me, of course, and kneaded my nightly transgressions into loaves of bread he could handle. He prayed with me and in tones of seriousness, I said the standard prayer for beginners and I was in the club, I thought.

○

In 1996, Billy Graham was on what was touted as his last crusade. I'd graduated from college seven years prior and any holy water dispensed those weeks in 1988 was rapidly evaporating. God's messengers still came for me at many venues and in many forms. They appeared on street corners; they appeared in bus depots and in airport rest rooms. On two occasions I found a solicitous pamphlet left in my gym locker with the self-effacing sincerity that a subliminal suggestion would require. It was as though I wore a sign on my forehead that read: **Bound for Hell.** Maybe it was there, but only my guardian angels who saw that I struggled with a disability could see it and when I looked in the mirror it faded. Such as a vampire can't see a reflection, that marking wasn't on my head at all for me to see. I concluded that it must have been just a figment of their self-righteously inclined imaginations.

○

"Mike, how have you been?"

"All right, I guess. Man, I haven't heard from you since college. What are you doing these days?" I asked, guessing his life had panned out better than mine.

"Well, we have one boy and another child on the way. My wife's in data entry and I'm in pharmaceutical sales," he replied quietly so as not to sound pretentious.

He had obtained a business degree while I merely had a liberal arts degree that offered fewer opportunities for lucrative employment. One really needs a master's degree to accompany the BA to put it to use. Contrary to what he would most likely claim as his key to success, I knew it was the degree he had chosen. It was the simple fact that he had the acumen for business while I refused to live my life thinking inside the box. I could hear him explaining to me that God had created me with right brain capacity while he was endowed with the incidentally more profitable left brain capacity. I was not married and even if I had been, I doubted I'd have wanted a family. Although these situational factors aside, I still did not discount the ubiquitous detail that he had put his life in the hands of a deity and was under His guidance.

"Billy Graham is coming to the Metrodome next month and I'd like you to come with us."

"I don't think so," I kindly replied on instinct.

"He is getting old and this may be the last crusade," he added to bolster his invitation.

I knew Graham was only seventy-eight and had many sermons left. Still my friend continued his crusade to create a sense of urgency to see the evangelist whose message I thought could only be repetitive and my attending would be disrespectful to the many that came to him whole-heartedly, devout in seeking God. I did, however, think he was the most sincere pulpit pounder out there. He lacked the flamboyant incredulity of the Jimmy Swaggarts or the Jim Bakers of the PTL "clubs." If I consented to hear the ramblings of any man of God, it would be Graham. I had looked into God's frosted windows from a dormitory and had sinned to tell about it. If it hadn't stuck there why did my friend think it would stick in the Metrodome? I figured the smaller and more improbable the setting; the more likely "magic" was to happen. The Teflon roof of the Metrodome had repelled some baseballs, a few heavy snowfalls and would most likely slip through the busy hands of God. My friend persisted. However, he never indicated that he'd judge me differently if my final decision was not to go.

"Mike!" He always said my name with an emphatically metered suggestion, surely designed to pique my curiosity. "Come with us to hear Billy. Check it out. My wife's seven months pregnant, but she's still going," he spoke plainly and nonchalantly, leaving me only a slowly tightening loophole through which I could reject his offer.

"I'll pass this time," I said with a dissonant temptation for what I might be missing festering at the back of my mind. He'd call again, I told myself. He did and I turned him down again. A few more calls were placed and all ended with me rejecting his offer of what was really nothing more than a wholesome form of entertainment. In college I'd been looking for answers and most of our encounters had occurred at my instigation. Now he was asking me. It became a game and I greedily sought the longevity of it. I needed to know how long until his auspices ran dry. I also found his reference to "the wife and kids" curious, unquestionably including his unborn child as a thriving member of his family. I determined that it was another Christian thing–to speak of the birth of a child as though it is imminent, and will come out of the womb alive and well. It occurred to me that he could have some prescience. One night, a week before the event, my friend called. I had a sense that this was my last opportunity to oblige. It was.

"Mike! I'll ask again. Do you want to join us to hear Billy?" His tone conveyed the frustration that a salesman must swallow on the dutiful road of persistence.

"Why not–sure, I'll go," I said, and thought of the hackneyed words I'd hear like they were propaganda films without spoiler alerts.

○

Turnstiles led into caged alignments as we filed into the dome. Those on crutches moved to the head of lines while the wheelchair-bound were ushered in by smiling, plain-clothed workers. There was no security and if any hostility had broached the sidewalk curb of the dome, it was graciously and willingly checked at the door. Alcohol did not lighten the mood or impair sensibilities that were there for a higher purpose. They came from all walks of life peacefully, lovingly, amiably, with a song in their heart and a lingering doubt in their brains that sought an answer. Singers highlighted by Amy Grant sang songs ripened with the same message, that there is hope in the world. It was a soft sell. No fire and brimstone conjuring allusions to hell found their way onto the stage that evening. It was a simple platform that assumed none of the grandeur that an 1850s tent revival may have deserved. Beneath the billows of Teflon hung with heavy lights, something happened that Elmer Gantry would have envied. After Graham had spoken for an hour, throngs of people seeking salvation were fed onto the field. I was a spectator to human magnets. There was a force, a steely man in the center of the field, to whom ordinary people were drawn. They walked in three lines, twenty abreast, from sections of the dome. Then I noticed the same thing was happening on our side. Three lines, in perfect formation, were born from the sections in which I sat. They went calmly, determinedly, perhaps with gullibility, but then skeptics may not live to regret their ignorance of folly. Graham stood vigilant as his chosen people came forward to claim their redemption. He stood awestruck as those in wheelchairs wheeled themselves slowly, arduously negotiating the AstroTurf covering the floor of the Metrodome. Each man, woman and child crowded before him, imbibing his words in silence. His arms reached out to figuratively touch each and every member who sought

His salvation by accepting the word. He reached out to every student or blue-collar worker who found that his or her life was going nowhere fast and had surrendered it to Jesus like I had facilely done six years before.

I did not go down on that field and I was not expected to go. Some Christians, whether they are born once or twice, are more sincere than others. Some genuinely do not have an ulterior motive in befriending you. But some are just more artful in their sales technique. They "spread the word," but hide it under so many layers of secular, user-friendly words that their protégé is caught before he can get away. In layman's terms, it is the bait and switch. My friend did not go down on the field either. His pregnant wife waddled down, though, to have her baby blessed by Graham. He pressed his hands on her belly and they both knew that the child was being born into a deeply Christian family.

After a suitable and convincing sojourn of truth, the pilgrims filed peacefully back to their sections in the same manner as they had come. Nothing had changed and the magic that I genuinely hoped to see was evidently never intended. By this I mean a staged illusion, the likes of a David Copperfield show, but even that did not happen. Graham said some more words about the lives of the people who had gone down to meet him and what they could now expect. There was some more singing, real, uplifting gospel, revival-type singing with the crowd clapping as their standing ovations morphed into dancing. I was smiling and dancing with them all. I, a Reform Jew who'd only had what amounted to an unsuccessful conversion to Christianity, was enthralled with the serenity and harmony of the event. Eventually the singers began to file out of the dome, although even exiting they created the illusion that they were still in full, fervent command of the stage. The music dimmed and the lights that hung from the Teflon went on and Billy Graham's disciples shined with the answers they'd found.

◯

I really wanted to see a change. I felt for those people who so desperately came there seeking one in their lives. I hoped that they got one and it lasted. My rational self knew though that, at best, these people were merely given strength to improve their lives that evening. They were also given the metaphysical power of people having a common goal, need, or want. I felt very good that I had witnessed Billy Graham who had been moving people toward a common goal for over half a century. As the pressure of the dome blew us out the doors opposite the turnstiles through which we'd passed, I looked back to see if I had missed any magic. Then I saw those on crutches and in wheelchairs being blown out, the latter spinning to a stop on the sidewalk in front of the dome. They were the same; nothing magically faded like when Forest Gump ran and gradually lost his braces through Hollywood special effects. The smiles were brighter though and those pilgrims were filled with hope, positivity, and a constructive attitude about their disability.

That was the magic to me.

The Burial Plot

The plane is full and my wife holds my hand. I look from my aisle seat across to the window. Baggage handlers heave and shove in clusters. Their end products go on a conveyor belt. I know somewhere in the underbelly of our DC-10 (or in the hold of another plane) is my grandmother. I glance back. A few rows away from to us, my dad sits with his wife. Always studious, with an insatiably hungry mind, his eyes fix on the in-flight magazine. I wonder what is going through his head. The flight magazines are always yesterday's news.

It is the first week of June 2003 and the sun grazes at the tarmac, foreshadowing the summer ahead. Oma (affectionate German for "Grandma") lived most of her senior years with her only immediate family, her son, my dad, in Minnesota. She first lived in an independent living facility in St. Paul's Highland Park area. Her independence dwindled and dad eventually moved her to a nursing home. My mom, my wife and I and dad, all have visited her on separate occasions. His wife visited Oma often and at times comforted her, holding her close in the final days. I remember going to the home in May with my wife. We sensed they were our last visits. Oma seemed to know this too. She looked so frail, and she stared at the ceiling with tenuousness to this world in her eyes. It was as though she saw something she could not share with us. I don't think anyone can see that look and not be the slightest bit curious about an afterlife.

Oma's husband, Opa (affectionate German for "Grandpa") passed away suddenly from a heart attack in 1968. At the time they were living in

Red Bank, New Jersey. I was three years old and remember best the jolting manner in which we got there. A mid-morning flight took us to Newark and then a small single-prop plane took us to Red Bank. Opa's sister, Beda, her second husband, Chil, and his daughter Mona also attended the funeral. I'm told a few of Opa's business associates attended. Peddlers he'd traversed South Jersey with showed up to pay their respects. I never knew Opa, although, I do know he was likely the first Amram to be buried at New Jersey's Beth Israel Cemetery.

Earlier in the week we met my sister, her husband and their two daughters in New Jersey. They'd driven down from Massachusetts. The occasion became a kind of reunion. It was a time to consider Oma while also bonding three generations. The eight of us checked in to a hotel near Woodbridge, New Jersey. The funeral was Thursday. We left the hotel a few times during the week, but mostly we bonded, shared memories and ordered room service.

A slight chill teased the air as we walked to the burial plot. A rabbi welcomed us all, offered his sympathies and hugged us like he knew us. His rekel (a long black coat, typically worn by Hassidic men), elusively brushed at his neck. He did his job with the superficiality to which emotion often concedes. His eyes crinkled and he davened (prayed rhythmically). He declined to stand (as is the custom) and rocked in his wooden grave site chair as he chanted the Kaddish prayer. He claimed to have an affiliation with the temple my sister worked at in Massachusetts. The reality was that he was an anonymous rabbi, but he worked his way into our minds to do his job. I guess that is a skill reserved for people who frequent God's auspices.

He davened madly, attacking the remaining strains of the Kaddish like a repentant vulture. A wooden casket waited on a wheeled device alongside a wide rectangular hole. Chanting resounded from its vacancy, and the wheeled cart brought the deceased closer to the hole. It was surreal, the kinetic powers that rabbi had. I watched closely and soon groundskeepers appeared. It was as though they had been hiding behind other graves. The belts holding the casket on the wheeled device were released. The keepers slowly guided Oma into the ground. Their timing was right. The Yiskor (memorial prayer) was completed just as the last corner of the casket touched the earth. The rabbi nodded and we each took turns throwing shovelsful of dirt into the hole.

According to the Gregorian calendar, Oma died June 1, 2003. This translates to the Hebrew month of Sivan, also on the first day, in the year 5763. Rabbinic wisdom dictates that Shiva (a seven-day mourning period) be ended early in the event it falls during one of the following Jewish holidays: Passover, Shavuot, Sukkot or Rosh Hashanah. The reasoning is that these days are a time of joy. We entered the gates of Beth Israel Cemetery on the fifth day of Sivan. Shavuot began the next day. By sundown that day, Shiva was ended. Dad is not Orthodox or spiritual. He practices a quite liberal Reform Judaism. He wore the tallis (prayer shawl) as a Bar Mizvah for his parents. A loophole was provided by Jewish law. Dad did not feel remiss at all about not sitting Shiva for his mother.

¶

The ship carrying Oma, Opa and their son, Manfred (dad) arrived in the shadow of the Statue of Liberty November 15, 1939. Oma had arranged for their departure from Germany. She obtained a sponsor, HIAS (Hebrew Immigrant Aid Society), and in late October of 1939 they left. They came to America, via Holland and Belgium, from Hannover, Germany. Upon entering America, Meinhardt (Opa) became Milton and Manfred became Fred. Sitta—for reasons that had much to do with what she'd escaped—remained Sitta.

Freddy grew up in an Orthodox Jewish house. He went to Hebrew school to become a Bar Mitzvah in 1946. His maternal grandmother, Omi (Else), lived with Oma, Opa, and him in their Manhattan apartment. Omi kept kosher with great piousness. When she visited us in Minnesota, my mom had two sets of dishes for her. One set was for her beef and the other for dairy. Oma lacked the conviction of her mother.

Freddy enrolled at Syracuse University in upstate New York in 1951. Opa had been working for many years as a peddler, procuring anything that a housewife could need. He commuted from their 77th Street apartment in Manhattan to his route in towns in South New Jersey such as Freehold and Long Branch. Sitta and Milton left New York in 1958 and settled in Red Bank, New Jersey. Else Nussbaum (née Muller), Sitta's mother, resided in a nursing facility in the New York borough of Queens.

¶

Else Nussbaum stood 4 feet 11 inches. "Omi" is another affectionate German word for grandma. It could be diminutive, denoting size, and, in this case, was quite fitting. The name also served to differentiate her from Freddy's paternal grandmother, Jettchen, whom he called Oma. Sitta and her mother moved to Miami, Florida, in 1970. Omi was frume (Jewishly observant), and a kosher nursing home was imperative. The one that was found was located in South Miami. My Oma had already settled in an apartment in North Miami.

Oma needed to be in the "proper" part of Miami. Her home was kept immaculate. Everything had its place. Pillows were never overstuffed (like Freddy used to love at Aunt Beda's apartment). Oma left nothing to chance. Shoes were not allowed across the threshold. Spotless from the door onward, was maroon, mauve and brown carpeting. It proceeded flush to the walls and was as soft as velvet. Area rugs were islands where floor was unprotected. I'm guessing the only time the carpet needed to be vacuumed was after we visited.

Sitta had a subtle elitist streak. She thought Polish Jews were beneath her in status. Beda's second husband, Chil, fell into this category. It was largely for this reason that she disparaged Beda. Growing up, Freddy was neither encouraged nor discouraged from spending time with his only aunt. Beda passed away in 1977. She was buried next to her first husband in Beth Israel Cemetery. I am told that Oma refused to attend her funeral.

Oma visited Omi religiously. She rode the bus to South Beach and kvetched (complained) about it. In the last years of Omi's life, their relationship was co-dependent. I saw Omi in about 1977. The nursing home smelled of urine and anti-septic sprays. She was frail and her smile was apprehensive and toothy. Her hair was wild and brittle. I felt her loathing, even if she didn't. She gripped her wheelchair tightly, precariously covered by an orange and brown Afghan. Omi passed away in the nursing home October 1, 1980. She was ninety-four. Her body remained in Florida and was buried in the city of Doral at Lakeside Memorial Park.

¶

Oma had tried to negotiate the sale of Omi's plot at Beth Israel long before Omi's death. The plot in the cemetery was one site over from her own and Opa's. It did not sell. The plot was worth only a few hundred dollars, but Oma insisted on getting the money. The plot was listed for sale for years, and no one bought it. In the late 1990s, dad and his wife went to New Jersey to deal with the people at Beth Israel. The cemetery staff was rude and difficult so a decision was made to donate the plot. It went to people who could not afford to be buried in Beth Israel. Oma never knew the plot was given away. Ironically, it was donated for use by exactly the type of people on whom she would likely look down upon, in life and death.

¶

Jewish law dictates the deceased never be unattended before burial. A shomer (guardian) is assigned to the body. Physiological laws make it impossible for a human to ride in an unpressurized belly of an airplane. Omi would have had to be driven to Woodbridge from Miami (1,256 miles) to observe the Jewish law and still end her life as piously as she had lived it. It is doubtful this law was ever considered, however. Still, a truly spiritual person might say the decision on where Omi would rest was influenced divinely. She remained in Miami, was never unattended and left this world with a piousness that was as spotless as the carpet in Oma's apartment. More likely Omi was buried in Florida because Oma did not want to pay to transport a body. Also, Omi's space at Beth Israel was listed for sale at the time of her death.

A rabbi once told me funerals are for the living. Surely the spirit world supersedes earthly logistics. Oma passed away in the St. Paul nursing home where she'd lived the last years of her life. The funeral home she was taken to observed Orthodox Jewish custom. Regardless of the living's religious sentiments, the customs were carried out in full. They were included in the price and Oma's body was attended by someone from the time she entered the funeral home to the time she was put on the plane. The decision to transport her to New Jersey was morally motivated. The living had to live with their decision. Oma claimed she did not want anyone to bear the expense of transporting her. There was no directive stating this. Even if there were, sometimes moral obligations contradict anything written with a sound mind in a law office. Dad guessed it was his mother's "secret wish" to be buried in New Jersey next to Opa.

¶

My sister—an educator at a temple in Massachusetts—officiated at the unveiling. This is the ritual of presenting the Matzevah (tombstone) at a second ceremony, up to a year after the burial. It is not in the Halakha (Jewish law) but came to be a tradition by Jews in the latter half of the nineteenth century. It is done within the year following the funeral, but no less than six months after. It had been roughly nine months since Oma's funeral. Woodbridge's ground was allowed to settle. The eight of us gathered once more at Beth Israel April 18, 2004. Customary prayers were read. A kaddish was said, preceding words of my sister's own devise.

We were all given a few moments to share memories of Oma after which, in a Jewish custom, we tossed pebbles on the headstone embedded in the ground. Strands of dead grass wisped over the name, assuring us of their green rebirth as the season changed.

Oma and Opa were together again. I witnessed their headstones side by side. They were together in dad's mind. They'd forever be together in that cemetery. Dad insists he's not spiritual. Although, if there is ever any doubt in his mind whether his mother wanted to be buried in New Jersey, he can rest easy—and she can as well. Oma had purchased that plot for herself. Obviously she fully intended Beth Israel Cemetery to be her final resting place. Dad fulfilled Oma's wish and gave himself peace of mind.

Jews observe a yahrtzeit, a memorial, during which a candle is burned, tzedakah (charity) is given and prayers are read. Tradition dictates yahrtzeits be observed on the Hebrew date of passing. Such annual remembrances are done for Milton (30th day of Av), Sitta (1st day of Sivan), and Else (21st day of Tishrei). Traditional Jews, if spiritual, know and appreciate Olam Ha-Ba as an afterlife or a world to come. In Judaism the focus is the here and now. Jews are not always living for the future. Any belief system regarding an afterlife is not binding and ample room is given for personal opinion. Orthodox Jews may believe that the souls of the truly pious ascend to a place similar to the Christian heaven. Perhaps it's a parallel universe. They also may give reverence to the theory that the departed are reincarnated through many lifetimes. There is the belief that the messiah will come and the dead will be resurrected. In this case, if the deceased believed in an afterlife and if at least one of the people observing the yahtzeit believes in one, it is a safe bet Oma, Opa, Omi, Beda, even Chil, are all together.

The Genuine Article

*L*ucy called her cousin's mother Tenna. The name was a contrivance of the German relation aunt, which is *Tante*. It always came out of her mouth slowly, painfully phonetic, with young Lucy tripping over the T as she began. Tenna (Haika) Tannenbaum lived on a fixed income in a co-op. She owned half of a Victorian-era apartment building bordering the south side of Central Park that she had purchased in her youth. She and Lucy took long, long walks in the park, often passing the patch of ground that said "Imagine" swimming in mosaic pieces.

On the night of May 17 RAF Hampdens began a bombing raid on oil installations in Hamburg. The Tannenbaums had come from Eimsbüttel, a borough of Hamburg, Germany. Hamburg had become a *Gau*, one of the de facto administrative divisions of Nazi Germany. When the British air raids began, the Tannenbaum parents left with Haika, her brother, Gerd, and their maid, Anna. They arrived in New York Harbor in June of 1940.

In the beginning of Hitler's rule in 1933, there was no clear method of defining who was Jewish. Within the next two years, the Nuremburg laws cleared up any misconceptions with regards to race. The laws deemed people with four German grandparents as "German, or kindred blood," while people were said to be Jewish if they descended from three or four Jewish grandparents. A person with only one or two Semitic grandparents was considered to be a *mischling*, a crossbreed of mixed blood. Margot Tannenbaum's mother, Hannah Schwartz, had married a man named

Herschel Lipchitz. Marcus Tannenbaum was raised by a woman who was descended from Russians and a father with Austrian ancestry.

The gene pool was shallow and tiny *kepot* (skull caps) tread hard in the bloodstream, trying to survive. In 1935, upon tracing the Tannenbaum's lineage back further, it became less Aryan. The Tannenbaum family's concern about the Nazis would become progressively less. Because of Haika's grandmother, Oma Lipchitz and Dr. Tannenbaum's mother's Jewish ancestors from Russia, Haika and her family fell under the heading of *mischlinge*.

Φ

Tenna's daughter, Freda, bit her nails nervously as she watched young boys play with their sail boats in the pools in Central Park. She was out on a walk with her mother. Fraulein Tannenbaum could no longer drive herself and had given Freda her red 1958 Cadillac. Freda drove from Queens each week to visit her mother.

The Catholicism the Tannenbaums followed in Hamburg had failed to work its magic on Haika. She strayed far from it and never married the man who finally confessed to being Freda's father. Freda barely knew her father who, by her calculations, had conceived her in the spring of 1958. Freda was now 32, the same age as the red Cadillac, and her mother was 65. The story Freda was told as a child went like this: Haika was at a party one spring night in the late '50s when she met a nice young Jewish man of Polish extraction. Haika had left her parents' upscale home on Staten Island years before to live in a one-room apartment in Greenwich Village. It was the height of the beat era and she usually was stoned out of her mind or lost in the poetry of Allen Ginsberg or William Burroughs. She wore her shiny blonde hair loose or spilling out from under a beret. Her blue eyes were deep pristine wells that ached to confess her past. Her clothes were always simple–dirty denim overalls often covered a chest that was otherwise bare. She was not modest and often went shirtless under her overalls on hot summer nights. Since she had not been created with much in the way of a bust, she felt the comfort a man might feel going around bare-chested and lifting arms with an uninhibited flare to show her unshaven arm pits. She was a free spirit, adamant on torturing her parents for forcing her to adhere to a strict Catholic upbringing.

Φ

Maybe God did know better after all. Eight weeks after a poetry gathering, Haika urinated to successfully germinate the eggs of an African claw frog. Her primal instinct told her to hop a train to Mexico to have the fetus eviscerated manually. The impulse quickly subsided, partly because she knew doing so would drive a permanent wedge between herself and her mother, but mostly because of the risk to her own life and the distinct reality of the creation of another. Soon the process of fingering the father began. Four men were candidates for father's day–two of Jewish extract and two of Anglo-Saxon extract. She chose one of the Jews after the baby was born and she matched his blood type against the baby's and eliminated three of the men. Her instincts weren't proven wrong. She had inadvertently reversed the trend toward drowning the family's Semitic gene in the pool. The twosome had created a baby that was three-quarters Jewish. Haika, perhaps sub-consciously, had chosen Lek Valadski, a Pole, to further anger her parents.

Lek fathered Freda in absentia. All Haika knew was that he was living somewhere out West. After he'd been subpoenaed to produce his blood type and named as the father of a new strain of *mischling*, he packed up his bongos and unfinished poems and headed west. For much of her life, Freda thought she had no father and her mother had hung a for rent sign on her uterus. She once wondered whether Haika was even her mother and not a surrogate whose post-partum bonds had been allowed to take root. One spring day in 1974, Freda began to ask questions.

"Mother, how come you never married?"

102

"I suppose I never wanted to be tied down, dear. See, my observations have been that men, even if it's unintentional, have a way of stripping you of your freedom. If the government can't do it, then the man gets impulsive and thinks that the job is his. I saw it happen to your Oma Margot and I always feared falling into the same trap," she replied thoughtfully.

"Well, I know what it takes to make a baby, so how did I get here?"

Haika thought quickly about what to tell her daughter as pangs of doubt went through her mind of her decision to lobby for better sex-education in the New York schools. There was no kosher recourse—she had to formulate some plausible explanation that would satisfy the laws of biology.

"Sweetheart, it was a crazy time in the 1950s. Everyone was trying to have sex with no babies coming at the end." Freda looked confused and Haika sighed. "You know, just for fun."

It was the age old conflict of sex for procreation vs. recreational sex, and Freda hadn't experienced either.

"Let me put it this way, if there is a god, it was meant for that sperm to meet my egg that night. If not, you might say it was a statistical accident—fortunate, but still statistical," she instructed her daughter.

"Mother, if you don't know there is a god, how is it we get up each morning with hope for the future? I think I believe in God. I believe in something that keeps the optimism."

"Well, you're lucky … I guess. Let me tell you a story,"

Freda smiled in anticipation of one of her mother's uplifting tales.

"In 1940 the Allies began to bomb us relentlessly. The British were dropping them and setting Hamburg on fire. For days on end, your Uncle Gerd and I had to stay in shelters. I wanted to know who it was. Who was it that had angered people so much that they would retaliate with such force? I soon learned from newspapers that it was a little man named Adolf Hitler that was going around Europe doing unthinkable things to human beings. For me the idea of God died there. But our house was very much

Catholic. When we were able, we went to church, even catechism. I refused to believe a god could be looking out for our best interests and still allow a man like Mr. Hitler to cause all that destruction of property and human life. I compromised. I told myself I would believe if I was provided with knowledge that led me to conclude that a superhuman entity was looking out for good. I did not know God was there when my small world was exploding in front of me, and I still don't today as young men come off planes in body bags and the most common use of an American flag is to drape over a coffin."

"You paint a bleak picture, mother. You have to believe something in spite of it all, don't you?"

"I just couldn't. I didn't have it in me. I lacked that blind faith most children inherit regardless of how the world treats them. I needed proof and I made a promise with myself that I would believe in a loving god if something magical or super-human were to appear to me someday."

"So, what if you picked up the paper tomorrow and the headline read Vietnam War Ended–would you make good on your promise?"

"No, I wouldn't. I'd just attribute it to the years of protest and wiser heads finally prevailing. The fact would remain that countless lives were lost for nothing."

"Then please tell me what would it take for you to have a concrete belief in God?"

"Let's see–say a Ferris wheel was stuck and we were in the top car. The car broke from its hinges and went plummeting to the earth. Moments before it hit, a hand, or something larger than our minds allowed us to comprehend, scooped us up and averted any injury to us. If that happened–and I was sober–I would have no choice but to believe in a higher power that defies all human logic."

"But mother, why did it save us and not the little boy drowning in a pool somewhere we might read about the next day?'

"Maybe we were lucky. Perhaps our combined lives were worth more than the boy's."

"What does Uncle Gerd think about these things?"

"It did not take much for him. A few trips to church and bombed-out Sunday school class rooms, and he had washed his hands of the whole thing. Your uncle is a die-hard atheist. My brother never gives any thought to the fact that there might be a god somewhere."

"You're sure of your own resolves though? You'd swear on your mother's life," Freda goaded.

"Yes. That's the deal I made. But since I left Hamburg in ruins, the world has done nothing to show me anything better."

"Okay, mother, but what about babies being born? Doesn't that suggest there's something higher possessing some knowledge that we don't have?"

Haika looked out the window at children playing in Central Park. They were truly amazing, how oblivious they seemed of the world's present or past problems. All they cared about was sailing their boats straight and keeping them afloat. But there were so many of them—boats and children. She swallowed hard and looked away from the window.

"Sweetheart, with every child born the novelty weakens. Science has answered who, what, when and how. All that remains is why it happens—why combining an egg with one sperm out of a million can evolve into a human being. I guess agnostics and atheists just kind of take the 'miracle' of birth for granted. However, now women have a choice of whether we want to use our ability to make babies. We have some control over the process. The man is no longer calling the shots. If we choose not to let the fetus possibly thrive inside for nine months, we now can have the process stopped with much less risk to our own life."

"So then if you woke up today and found that you were pregnant with what could be me you might give abortion more consideration."

Freda probed deep, following her mother's eyes for a trace of submission. Her mother looked evasively out the window. Freda had struck a chord that was lost, but not forgotten. Sunlight streamed in Haika's eyes and she squinted wearily as she was taken to the mat. She sighed and looked her daughter in the eyes.

"I would have had a baby," she finally said and busied herself with her plants in the window.

Φ

In the spring of 1987, the ducks returned to their rightful place in Central Park with the older children having become proficient at navigating their boats around them. Haika watched them meticulously from her east window, panning the rising suns that sprawled across the water. She looked for greatness and the overcoming of timidity or adversity. She critiqued the boats and the technological advances to which the young sailors had adapted. Simpler times had lost. Hand-held electronic games often won the battle of what to lend the most dexterity and focus.

On one of Freda's trips to the city she complained to her mother that she had only seen a few pictures of Lek through the years. He was a short man with a scraggly beard and a balding head. She imagined him bald with hats to protect him from the sun's cancerous effects. He had brown eyes and sharp, wiry, sandy blonde hair that circled his head and miraculously found his beard. Haika never looked at the photos with her daughter, giving her the hint that the subject of a father not be discussed frequently. When Freda was a teenager, she began to ask questions.

"Mother, did I ever have any encounters with Lek that I can remember fondly?"

"Well, when you were about four he called me up and said I have to come down to D.C. to hear Martin Luther King. It was lovely and very hot and the August sun blazed across the reflecting pool to shine on the Lincoln Memorial. As Dr. King stood at its base to deliver his "I Have a Dream" speech, you wiggled out of Lek's arms and we spent the duration of the seventeen-minute speech chasing you through some 300,000 people.

When we finally found you, you had worked your way down to the end of the pool where you were dancing to Peter, Paul, and Mary as they sang *If I Had a Hammer*. I remember Lek saying, 'That's one gutsy kid we made.'"

Freda imagined herself enveloped in throngs of protesters, oblivious to the significance of the event and intent on satisfying her own curiosity. She saw a little girl dancing, pumping her arms wildly with carefree innocence.

"Your Uncle Gerd was there with his girlfriend and their daughter Lucy. Your cousin was only one and a half and spent most of the time sucking on her mother's breast. Your Tante Natalie is generously endowed and not modest at all," she added jealously. "Oh, they were so cute ... Lucy clad in sheepskin diapers and her mother wearing a papoose and very short shorts, gently swaying to the music."

"Anything else?"

Like a defense attorney, Freda berated her mother for evidence of her father's love.

"Not really. That was the only time I ever saw him really show concern for you. And even then he might have just been caught up in the harmonious feeling. There was a feeling that slid across that pool from the memorial that day. It was palpable—hot and sticky, uncomfortable in the heat that our closeness brought, but I knew everyone felt it."

"Really, in twenty-eight years, that's it! Just one show of any father-daughter bond?"

Her voice quivered and tears choked inside. Freda suddenly realized that her mother had raised her entirely alone and harbored a lot of resentment towards Lek. She got the feeling that her mother did not think of him much at all and that her reminding her of him must be painful.

"Do you mind talking about him?"

"Well, it's not my favorite subject, but you have a right to know."

She looked out over the wall that surrounded the east end of the park. She watched the children still reeling in their boats.

"See, your father got a degree in some computer-related field in the mid-'70s and got a job with a big computer company. That was the last time I heard from him. He never gave me an address or anything. That's all I know.

"Freda, would you be accepting of him if he suddenly called you?"

"Probably."

"Really, after he abandoned you?"

"Mother, eleven years have gone by since he moved and maybe he's changed. Maybe he's afraid to call thinking I'll blow up at him if he does."

Freda closed her eyes. Sun funneled to them through the bay window. Haika sighed, proud of her daughter's mature attitude.

"You know, Freda, I hated him with a vengeful passion for many years. But it turns out that the one lesson I actually took away from all that bible study is the one of forgiveness. Of all the things that collection of worthy parables has to offer, that has jumped out at me as the one that could benefit humanity the most. I don't think perpetually hating someone does anyone any good. He did what he did then for whatever reason he needed to at the time. It's done–gone and never can be rectified in any way that would really soothe the initial wound. So why let it fester and crowd the rest of life? Why let it become something that might sub-consciously be projected on other people?"

She sat down and began to massage her leg.

"Are you all right mother?"

"Just a little arthritis. I'm fine."

"Do you have pain often?"

"When I stand for long periods, my legs start to tingle. A doctor said it might be a thrombosed vein. He gave me a blood thinner and told me to keep off my legs," she hung her head and spoke casually.

"Are you trying to find a job where you can sit down more often?"

"Well, I told the managers at the museum of my condition. I am in consideration for an administrative position."

Freda worked at Roosevelt hospital's emergency room in admissions and sat at a computer terminal all day. Her job was routine and she had burned out several years before. The last day she could recall actually feeling some enthusiasm for the job had been one December night in 1980. She shivered as she remembered the sudden blast of cold off Ninth Avenue as the ER doors swung open and John Lennon was rushed in on a gurney. She remembered his pale, sunken face and the holes that had been ripped in his body by hollow-point bullets. She recalled this tragic, sudden death and wished her mother could have her job. She would gladly take hers as a curator at the Museum of Natural History. Freda's legs showed no veins and her blood flowed freely, internally and externally. A thrombosis could potentially kill her mother. Clotting, as she bled from wounds, was life-sustaining. Clotting as blood flowed within her was life-threatening.

Φ

Whatever had spirited Haika through life had strayed far from bombed out churches of Hamburg. The suggestion of a god eluded her on a yearly basis. The idea of one had been re-visited twice in recent memory—once in regards to Freda's conception and once on a hot day one August when a dream was voiced for equality. The fleeting tranquility and joy each event brought was suggestive of a super-human director of the universe. Freda studied the few religious books her mother had when she was young. She was given the same chance to become a Catholic that her mother had. She fast became aware of the litany of guilt that often surfaces and becomes counter-productive to the faith. Freda had made her own decision by the time she was twenty. Catholicism was a hard sell and she'd willfully spent a month in a private girls' parochial school in 1972.

Φ

A private girl's school lay sequestered in the village of Hinshire. It was a day's train ride from the city, in the Diocese of the suburb. Her time in the academy diminished any interest she had in religion or subsequent belief in

God. The nuns smacked her on the wrists–occasionally other places–with a ruler for minor transgressions. She was tortured, both physically and mentally. Once, on a night before the Christmas holiday, a nun quietly slipped into her dorm room.

"Freda, I didn't see you in mass today. You do know Christmas Eve is tomorrow?"

"Yes, I do Mother Superior."

"Why weren't you there?"

Freda trembled. Her eyes drifted over the snow that had shaped the landscape of the Commons. Her mind never came. They couldn't adjust to the light.

"Earth to Freda," the nun smiled.

Her uniform skirt was hot in the over-heated dormitory. She squinted the sun to fit her world.

"Answer me!"

I–um--I had some last minute packing. I really did not think I'd be missed. No offense, Mother, but I find all this kind of boring. It's just not for me. I wasn't cut out for it. Some are, and that's beautiful," Freda said with a catch in her voice.

"Yes, and God understands. But I don't! You are confined to your dorm for the next two days."

"But I already purchased a train ticket. My mother expects me tonight. Please!"

The nun gave Freda a consoling look and left the room. Her eyes adjusted to the light, but there was nothing worth seeing anymore. No anticipation, no salvation.

Φ

Freda repressed her experience at the parochial school, but drew her conclusions from it. She regretted her decision to attend and often wondered if her mother even cared that she'd gone. When she came home she never explained her detention. She told her mother she did not want to go back and remained truant until she went back to the New York public schools that fall. She concluded then that God didn't care whether she was with her mother for Christmas. Freda never knew God and followed in her mother's nimble footsteps that danced around immortality.

Haika never communicated much with her brother. Gerd was a distant uncle who had last arrived when Freda was ten to extract a quarter from her ear. He'd moved from Buffalo to Liverpool in upstate New York in the early '80s. Gerd had moved away from his parents in 1965. He needed to distance himself from the wealth, erudite lifestyle and demands of his father. He purchased a one-way ticket on the Staten Island ferry, took his three-year-old daughter Lucy and made a new life. Lucy's mother lived in Woodstock, about 100 miles north of New York City, and met Gerd and her daughter at the ferry. Her days of traveling to see her daughter were finally over and they were one happy family. The Tannenbaums insisted on having one of their grandchildren under their supervision and possible religious influence. Marcus Tannenbaum, as a retired surgeon, rarely came in to the city. He had an administrative position on the board in the department of surgery at St. Lukes-Roosevelt Hospital. He never got past the fact that Lucy was born out of wedlock, but still lavished his wealth on his granddaughter.

Φ

"Uncle Gerd! Happy New Year!"

Freda hugged him, making him feel self-conscious as she pressed against his lanky frame. He noticed how his niece had developed.

"Haika, are you sure she's yours?"

"Kind of inappropriate, Gerd. Where's that woman I saw you with at the March on Washington? Hers was big enough for both of us. Do you ever think if there is a creator that he might give women like that too much up there and then not have enough for people like me?" she queried jokingly.

"Oh, we had a fight and she didn't want to come down. She hates the city."

"Are you still living together?"

"Oh yeah," he quickly affirmed.

"Something's rotten in upstate New York," she rolled her eyes. "Lay it on me."

Gerd resented his younger sister's meddling in his life. He'd left an over-protective mother to smother his father on Staten Island. Marcus had raised his children with a criticism that overshadowed the mothering his wife gave. Nothing Gerd ever did was good enough and punishments were frequent and hard. He frowned, accepting that his kid sister had resolved to mend his ways.

"We just can't live together anymore. The more I try to please her, the more she pushes me away. Get this—last night she said I apologize too much and I should work on my self-confidence!"

"Well, who are you trying to please? I never felt I filled daddy's coffers, but I did not care. I live my own life. What do I care if it's not good enough!"

"Natalie's more the Bohemian sort. She paints and writes a lot of angry poetry—oddly angrier now than stuff she was writing before she met me, now that I think about it. Father and mother never approved of her, mostly because she had no intention of ever marrying me. They also thought her artsy ways would influence me the wrong way. Are you still working at the museum?"

"Yes, but I am trying to get in a position where I can sit more of the day."

"Oh, what's wrong?"

"I might have a deep venous thrombosis in my legs."

"Sounds serious."

"And you, are you still toting that barge?"

"No, I retired from working on the Erie Canal in '85, bought myself an Apple computer and started an online art business. Art, poetry–really anything creative people want to sell." He paused, hoping his sister might ask questions and show her approval. "Well, It hasn't really been that profitable, but I think 1997 will be my year."

"I hope it is. So it is not your art; it's other people's, and you sell it for them?"

"Precisely… think of my little house in Liverpool as a brokerage house."

He envied Haika for her job at the museum. It was not glamorous, but was respectable and was not a dead-end. His parents accepted and respected their daughter's work even though they were upset by her lifestyle. Gerd had neither the lifestyle nor the profession to gain their respect. Dr. Tannenbaum had pulled strings to get Freda her job at Roosevelt Hospital and it bothered Gerd that his father did nothing to help him, aside from paying most of the cost of sending Lucy to Sarah Lawrence College. In 1985, she began a graduate program in pursuit of an MFA in writing during which she interned at *The New Yorker*. By the time she was thirty, she'd sold a few stories, articles and cartoons to the magazine. Gerd envied his daughter's tenacity in ascending to a magazine that was elitist enough to win his father's approval.

"So Gerd, how do you make any money at your art business?"

"Oh, well I charge a twenty percent fee."

"How many clients do you currently have?"

"Sixty, but I'm hustling more," he quickly added.

"Uh-huh," she nodded slowly and quickly turned to Lucy. "And how's my favorite niece?"

"Good, Tenna. I got my own column with *The New Yorker* last year!"

"Congratulations Lucy, that's wonderful!"

"Thank you Tenna," she smiled, and glared at her father.

Gerd found few words to praise his daughter's accomplishments, but lived vicariously through them. Haika sympathized with her older brother even though her parents didn't. She had always known how her father faulted Gerd for his lack of ambition and delusions of complacency in life. Mrs. Tannenbaum had done well over the years to improvise a guise of sympathy, but under it still laid the cold judgment of condemnation.

Φ

"Please pass the lasagna Tenna."

Margot knew that she could rely on her only daughter to bring the family together. The Tannenbaums–or a semblance of them–gathered at Haika's Central Park apartment the first weekend of each new year. It was a tradition that had begun in the early 1960s. Always on the agenda was the assessment of the previous year. People talked about their accomplishments. As was true this year, the elder Tannenbaums rarely found the inclination to attend, and each meeting ended leaving a sense that a god was not yet worthy of belief.

"Haika, do mother and father ever visit you here?"

"Daddy may contact me when he comes in to the hospital. Other than that I never hear from either of them. I can't even remember when I saw mother last," she shrugged as she stretched her legs under the table and wiggled them. She coughed and thumped her chest.

"Are you all right, mother?"

"I'm feeling a little d-d-diz ..."

"Mother!"

Gerd jumped to the phone and dialed 911. "Come quickly, my sister's just passed out. I can barely feel a pulse and she is very pale. We're at 1124 W. 98th St. in Manhattan!"

"What's happening to my mother!" Freda screamed.

"We'll know for sure when the paramedics arrive. I think she's had some kind of stroke," Gerd tried to stay strong as he comforted his niece.

"Please don't die mother, oh, please," she begged.

Haika's eyes were wide and glazed and her tongue wagged out of her mouth. Lucy applied some cold towels to Tenna's head as the siren got closer. It was shrill and final, as though a mystery was about to be uncovered. Gerd called Dr. Tannenbaum and described his sister's condition. Marcus said the prognosis wasn't good. His daughter had experienced a cerebral event. Tenna had arrived at Roosevelt Hospital's emergency room a faux simile of Haika Tannenbaum. The bubble caused by the thrombosis had reached her brain. Only Marcus was sure his daughter could never walk this earth again.

The family followed the gurney into the ER where everyone paused and looked helplessly at each other. Haika had tendered a health care directive stating that no heroic efforts were to be made in the event she could not sustain life on her own. Gerd bowed his head and nodded. The doctors obliged. She lay in a bed with electrodes trailing from her head to display brain activity on an EEG (electroencephalogram) monitor.

They all waited patiently at her bedside and studied her face for a sign of life. Dr. and Mrs. Tannenbaum each mechanically crossed their heart three times and began their silent dialogues. Gerd and the Tannenbaum grandchildren looked like they wanted to believe in something less tangible than a statistic. Lucy loved her Tenna and envied her unique brand of spirituality. Haika was spiritual in the sense that she thought love was a constant thing. It was in everyone, somewhere, even if they couldn't know it until they died and went on to the next world. It may have even been in the people who had angered the British enough to bomb Hamburg. She'd been impressed by the eastern religions that she thought had more plausibility. They were not designed with human flaws that cause guilt and self-doubt and justify things that are contradictory to a harmonious world. She had a willingness to accept new light, were it to rise in her lifetime. It hadn't, and Freda respected that. She remembered the conversation she had with her mother years ago about how knowledge could change some people and for others it was just an accident; be it happy or sad, it was only an unexplainable occurrence that remained a mystery to them. She looked at her grandparents and then at her cousin. Lucy had a blankness in her eyes that now fixated on the EEG monitor. She looked for signs of brain activity, glimmers of life on which she could base her hopes. Her grandparents had a twinkle in their eyes, but somewhere they knew that the reality was they'd lost their daughter. She'd passed on before them at a youthful sixty-six.

"Please come back Tenna," Lucy pleaded.

She shifted her attention from the EEG screen to her aunt's pale, callow face. Swirls of white-blonde hair fell on the pillow while conspiring to strangle her face. The hairs were aged and brittle and looked as though the brief time elapsed had been an eternity for them. Her hands lay at her sides relaxed, peaceful as though they wanted to teach one last lesson to her niece.

"OH MOTHER, YOU CAN'T DO THIS! DON'T LEAVE ME."

Freda wiped her eyes three times and stooped to hug her mother. She waited for Haika to hug back and Dr. and Mrs. Tannenbaum watched their granddaughter with loving pity in their eyes. To them, the loss was consolable. God had plucked their daughter from this earth and sent her on her way– hopefully to a better world. Marcus knew the intricacies, complexities and resilience of the human body. He also knew of the abrupt traumas from which it can never return. Margot clutched her husband's sleeve. Her eyes wandered around the hospital room as she followed Haika's spirit in its meanderings. She prayed God would remember her as an infant in Hamburg being baptized. Margot cried for her daughter and regretted their estrangement.

"My *kleine* Haika, I hope you are happy now, wherever you are. You never seemed happy in this world. Maybe our stations will meet one day and you will see things as they are."

Dr. Tannenbaum glanced up, noticing a slight jump in the flat line that darted anomalously across the EEG screen.

Certificate of Death

This is to acknowledge the death of
Haika Greta Tannenbaum
on the 4ᵗʰ day of January in the year of 1997
At: 02:15 eastern standard time
Signed: James Sammules, M.D.

Φ

"Haika said she wanted to be cremated."

"That's unacceptable, Gerd! Unless it is stated in her will, we will give her a proper Catholic funeral!"

"No, mother. You have pressed your opinions on me all my life. I'm not going to let my sister get gawked at by strangers. Who knows what kind of people would show up for such an event?"

"Gerd, how can you talk to your mother that way? Besides, I doubt your father would pay for a cremation. If it turns out we are legally bound to send her off that terrible way, we are not paying a dime."

"I'm not worried. Haika had a $10, 000 life insurance policy that will cover the cremation and an elegant urn."

"Are you sure she kept up the premiums? Knowing Haika, she probably let it get canceled."

"No, it's good. She was very good about keeping up with that."

Gerd beamed because he had proved his mother wrong. Margot sighed and answered the door.

"Marcus, what did the attorney say?"

"Well, we must honor her wishes to be cremated. So, Gerd, the ball's in your court now. Get to work, son!"

"Yes sir," he shyly obliged and was plagued with the same feelings of doubt that he knew from his youth.

Φ

May blossomed in the Village. Lucy and Freda had been planning a memorial party for months. It was not written in so many words in the will, but the inclination for levity over moroseness was implied. They had rented a café on McDougal Street for the event. People read poems, played bongos and folk music's lesser-known local acts played as God had intended them to play. Margot refused to go to the Bohemian event. Dr. Tannenbaum went and thought less of his wife for not joining him.

"Freda, is that you?"

"Lek, hello. It's been a while," she said unenthused.

"Sure has! Man, the last time we met, you were running around in diapers trying to break through security to meet Dr. King," he laughed, "You remember that?"

"Yes, that's the one memory I have of you."

"Come on Freda, I didn't expect you to run to me with open arms, but I had hoped for a little warmer reception than this."

Freda drank her beer in silence as aging beatniks read poems that hadn't changed with the times and still hoped for a world as it had been before the War in Vietnam. They nursed the dream while she drank— enough to sufficiently elevate her to a state her mother could see. She staggered off and left Lek wondering about her safety.

"Hey cuz, how are ya doin'," she said, slapping her back hard.

"I'm okay. It looks like you're enjoying yourself."

"I am so sorry for your loss Freda," interrupted Natalie. "Your mother was such a powerful spirit, I am sure she is in another world by now."

"Thank you, aunty–tante Natalie. Hey, how about just Tatalie," she laughed. "Cousin, I'd b-better be enjoying myself 'cause this type of event only happens once in a life–time. Well, one can only hope."

She composed herself and eased into her words. Natalie gave her daughter a hopeful look and left her to deal with her intoxicated babbling cousin. Life on McDougal Street thrived in ignominiously contrived patterns as they watched from the sidewalk. The promise of spring felt the sadness on their side of the street. But trees budded and birds sang and renewed energy flowed everywhere around them.

"Freda, do you think Tenna would like this?"

"Silly question. Of course she would! She'd have it just like this—a party like none before or after it to send her spirit screaming into the next life."

"Tenna used to tell me that when she was little and the Allied forces were bombing the blood out of the Germans was when she first lost her faith in a god. She compromised, though, and she said if the world ever showed her anything to prove there was a super-human being, she'd believe again."

Lucy's voice drifted off while Freda watched the guests step out of their cars. They arrived in twos and threes and stepped across the street fluidly.

"I always thought that was a fair deal. Unlike my dad, I'd like to give a god the benefit of our doubt."

Freda suddenly grabbed her cousin's hands and held them tightly. Her pupils were dilated and resembled tiddlywinks pieces that followed Lucy's eyes to the center of her soul. Freda flinched and her attention turned to the oblivious street life. Lucy watched in amazement as Tenna stepped out of her car. It was the old '58 Cadillac she'd given to Freda. Freda smacked herself several times to see if she was dreaming and then she smacked Lucy.

"I beg your pardon—what was that for?"

"Reality check," she said, rubbing Lucy's reddened cheek.

"Hey, I'm fine. Tenna's coming up the walk. See, I knew she wasn't dead."

Lucy smiled broadly in vindication while Freda shivered, waiting patiently for her mother to arrive. The other guests were unaware that anything extraordinary was happening. They kept toasting Haika's memory and reading poems that imagined a world in which such an occurrence might actually happen. She looked much younger than she was in January and had a spring in her step Freda had not seen since she was little. Gerd suddenly noticed her and his glass dropped on the walk.

"Good heavens … Haika? Father … father, come quickly."

He summoned Marcus away from a group of former colleagues.

"Yes, what is it son?"

"Haika is out there coming up the walk!"

"I knew those cigarettes smelled funny. Are you stoned out of your mind, son?"

"No, sir, I haven't had any. I might have a bit of a buzz from the beer, but I know what I saw."

Haika made her way into the café without arousing suspicion. She might as well have been a ghost because no one outside the family saw or heard her. The guests flapped their gums and ate a cake that was cut around a frosting image of her. Her friends appeared to have forgotten the reality of her loss after four months. She greeted a few people on her way through the crowd, but the music carried her voice away. It was folksy and vibrated through the crowd unnoticed. Harmonicas slid along lips pursed with promise of a better world and guitars were strummed to produce a steely, hollow squeak that sang songs in different pitches. Haika walked softly in a red, strapless dress she knew would infuriate her mother. Her steps were light–fleet, like those of a young woman who knew who she was and where she wanted to go. She wore red and white saddle shoes that made the wooden floorboards creak. She reached out to tap Dr. Tannenbaum on the shoulder.

"Haik …"

Marcus fell to the floor and she knelt down to revive him. The other physicians stood and stared down at the two Tannenbaums like a circle of deer that'd been caught in headlights.

"Daddy."

"How many of these have I had, Larry? Haika, *mien klienes Mädchen* (my little girl), I watched you die. Y-your ashes are in an urn with Lucy. That's it; I must be dead or dying."

Marcus lay back and relaxed at his revelation. He was ready to enjoy his trip to the Promised Land.

"Where's mother?"

"Still in Staten Island"

"She wouldn't come out for this?"

"No, too Bohemian. Are you very hurt?"

"No. I'm not surprised. Thank *you* for coming, though."

"Don't mention it. Why don't you pop in on your mother."

"What do you mean 'pop in?' What are you implying?"

Her voice rose in anger as she gently shook her father's withered mass. He rolled his head in confusion. His lips felt the words before they had come to his brain and came out automated.

"You appeared here, you can appear for your mother in Staten Island."

Haika looked up at the other doctors to see if they believed this. Some of them had left the circle and were sitting at the bar. She looked back down at her father in disbelief. She doubted he was dying.

"Don't be silly. I'll probably take the ferry out there."

"No, I think you should drive. I think your mother needs to see you now."

"Why? She hasn't made the slightest effort to see me in almost a decade, why would I bust my butt to see her?"

"Look around Haika—don't you see people are mourning your loss? They're eating cake around you!"

"Yes, it's a bit like a death mask though. Sure I'm flattered, but a little embarrassed. I did not get them anything. And why should I see mother? She did not even come to see me."

He slipped off, closed his eyes and pretended he was dead. A group of Haika's co-workers from the museum had gathered and scrutinized Dr. Tannenbaum as he lay in the middle of the café. She stood up and they noticed her dress was short and quite revealing. Her legs were smooth, shaved sheer and waited sublimely tanned under nylons.

"Haika, how are you? How's your leave of absence going? Are you ready to come back to work?"

"Sure, I'll be there Monday."

"Your legs look beautiful. You must have had that vein stripping you always talk about."

"Oh … yes, yes I did and I feel ten years younger. Thank you for noticing," she said and turned as red as her dress.

Haika was an unwitting *shiksa*. She'd devour oedipal men with the unconscious intent of angering her mother. Somehow the men knew she had fading Jewish roots suppressed in a ledger in a forgotten Nazi Genizah. Elliot Semmes had worked with Haika at the museum since she started. In all that time a spark of a relationship was savored but never allowed to ignite to anything more than a stroll through the park after work with the pretense of protection. Elliot was bolder than she had ever seen him. They were not at work, and the watchword sexual harassment was not omnipresent in his mind.

"Could I just feel your leg? It looks so smooth now."

"Sure, feel away. I'll stop you if you go too far," she cautioned and pulled up her dress slightly.

He closed his eyes and put his hand clumsily on her thigh and advanced it slowly up to the hem of her slip. She stopped him there, dead in his feel. It was a firm feel, a feel that knew she was alive and ready to go back to work.

"Thank you Haika," he smiled in satisfaction.

"You're always welcome Elliot. See you Monday."

Freda sat waiting for her mother to return. Empty bottles lined the table and Lucy wondered whether she should have paid for an open bar. The insurance money that was left paid for the party, mostly; Freda made up the difference. She had rarely seen her cousin drink in such excess. Freda basked in her inebriation which had now plateaued and she listened as a band covered Donovan's *Catch the Wind*. She sang out loud and poorly:

"In the chilly hours and minutes
Of uncertainty
I want to be
In the warm hold of your lovin' mind…"

It was beautiful and Freda sensed that the band had labored long to learn her mother's favorite song. It sounded effortless, but still it was obvious that it was not in the band's repertoire. Lucy stared at her cousin with a look that she was still not convinced of the beauty of the song or the band's ability to reproduce it so well. Freda sang more loudly as guests continued to leave.

"Cousin dearest, that's my mother's favorite song."

"You like it too?"

"Sure. Not as much, I guess," she shrugged. "I like Bob Dylan better. I once heard it said that Donovan was the British Dylan, but there will only be one Bob Dylan. I really like that stuff he put out in the late '70s–you know when he thought he was Christian for a while."

Haika stumbled out of the café lightly. Lucy just marveled at her Tenna and reached out to touch her hand. She squeezed it gently, but hard enough that both knew they were there.

"I missed you."

"Ah, that's sweet. I didn't go far. Are you enjoying your visit?"

Lucy nodded and looked at her cousin for affirmation. Freda was counting her bottles and took her mother's presence for the mundane occurrence it was. She'd drunk ten beers in the seven hours they had reserved the café. Her mother noticed the bottles she had lined up neatly like departed souls who were waiting to go into a new life.

"I don't recall you drinking that much Freda, dear. Anything on your mind you want to tell me?"

"Mother, do you remember that private school I went to when I was twelve?"

"Yes, I do. What brings that up? I thought you'd never speak of that again."

"Well, something happened while I was there, something awful that shattered any belief in God or anything super-natural ever happening. It happened just before Christmas that year."

"It must have been terrible. You never went back. Can you tell me?"

"It's not important what happened to me. I just want you to know that now I think those nuns were onto something. They were just human and had to do what comes inherently no matter how hard we try for something better."

Haika proudly stroked her daughter's thick red hair. Her hand weighed heavy on Freda's head and she knew no love had been lost between them. She smiled and gazed into her niece's misty eyes once more, probing them quizzically for signs of lingering doubt. A shadow remained and Lucy touched her Tenna's cheek with her index finger.

"What do you think Tenna, should we believe?"

"In God or miracles?"

"Doesn't one make the other possible?"

"Not all the time, depends whom you ask. Miracles happen all the time, but God is too busy to be there all the time. He gives us science and technology. That is usually enough to satisfy most people's curiosity. He only makes His presence known to the people that aren't satisfied," she calmly explained as she kissed her niece's finger.

"I love you Tenna. Don't ever leave me."

"When did I leave you?"

Freda jumped to her feet and hugged her mother. They went inside where the party was winding down, running out like a music box that's been wound to recollect a celebrated time in life. Gerd sat at the bar staring at his father who was lying on a couch in the middle of the room. Smells of funny cigarettes hung from the rafters. The words of eulogy and hopeful, transcendent poetry echoed from the walls. Remains of the cake lay in crumbs around the crooked smile of Haika's image. Her smirking mouth was like the largest island in the middle of a cake pan. Its smile mocked the event and made light of the effort and expense that had been made to honor her passing.

"Haika was never dead, father," Gerd finally concluded as he peeled at the label of his eighth beer.

"I saw her, son. I consulted with James Sammuels. I watched him sign the death certificate."

"I don't know what it was and don't really care what. Life will go on and people will die and some will live. It's that simple. No God, no miracles or magic. There's only accidents—happy and sad. Guess which this is?"

He leered back at his father lying on the velvet turquoise fainting couch. He envied his sister's ability to defy her parents, to always rise above them and somehow wiggle out of the traps that they set that had always caught him. This was no different. She'd done it again and bested their limiting, powerless expectations. She'd shoved their religion right in their faces and lived to see them faint.

"I don't think Haika's going to see Mother. Will you tell her about her return?"

"I don't believe I will Gerd … no, definitely not."

"Never?"

"I think knowledge of your sister's re-entry into this world would kill your mother. She's only hoping that your sister finds a spot in heaven—our heaven. No, your mother would never understand."

The party had exceeded its time and felt like Haika had orchestrated its longevity herself. The band was packing up to go home and the barkeep uttered last call. It was 2AM Sunday and the Tannenbaums were expected at their Staten Island church in seven hours. Marcus peeled himself off the couch and tested the firmness of the floor before he stood. All was well grounded and he prepared himself to leave the larger island for a smaller one. He went in the bathroom and splashed some water on his face and came out dripping wet.

"I'll see you sometime soon, maybe at the next family event," Dr. Tannenbaum said as he hugged his son. Gerd stood stunned as his father left the café. He had not seen such a display of affection since he was a boy in Hamburg. Haika stood smiling with open arms. Marcus hugged her quickly, barely making contact and nodded his farewell. He mumbled *aufwiedersehen* in a distant, native tongue. He hugged and kissed his granddaughters and sounded the locks on his Mercedes.

"Grandfather! Are you going to tell the priest about this tomorrow?" Lucy called. Marcus sighed, thinking he'd made a clean get away. He shook his head and slammed the door. The two generations of Tannenbaums watched as the third slowly pulled out of his space and drove away. Lucy looked up at her Tenna and shrugged.

"Tenna, I guess he couldn't handle it either. He couldn't explain it to the priest and won't even try. My guess is he wouldn't listen anyway and just go on preaching about God's work and the capable hands of Jesus."

"You're a smart girl Lucy."

She stroked her niece's cheeks, certain that she would use her new insight power responsibly.

"Freda, let's have brunch."

"You're staying mother? Going back to that same apartment by the park?

"Of course. Why wouldn't I? Where would I go?"

She studied her mother's features and realized how much alike the two of them looked. Now people could say they were sisters and it would not be hyperbole. They had rarely been as estranged as Haika and her mother, but Freda felt a strange sense of abandonment. It was like the empty feeling she felt whenever she thought of her father.

"Nowhere, I guess. Yes, I think brunch would be nice. I'll be in the city by nine."

"Did you want to join us Lucy?"

"No, thanks Tenna, I have things to do."

"Good seeing you again Haika!" Lek waved from his car.

"How long has he been here Freda?"

"Most of the party I think, I didn't see him much."

"That's too bad. You two could be closer sometime."

Her mother spoke in a tone Freda had never heard in the rare instances she spoke of her father. It was a voice that had no veil of anger, a voice like Lek had never hurt either of them.

"I'll see you tomorrow, then."

She kissed Haika and Lucy on their foreheads. Their senses were aware of the cool breeze that slowly dried their heads and ruffled their hair. Freda and Lucy watched Haika's Cadillac jolt to a start and speed erratically down McDougal Street. She had never been a good driver. Gerd and Natalie were never seen together at the party and now went their separate ways without even saying goodbye. Freda and her cousin said goodbye, hugged, and slipped into the echoing nightlife on the vacant streets of Greenwich Village. Each girl blazed a trail to her own subway station and descended.

Φ

The night was short and Lucy didn't sleep well. She showered and dressed and walked to the subway. It was a short ride from Bronxville to Mount Vernon. St. Paul's church had closed its doors for regular services in 1977, but Lucy liked to go there to sit and meditate. Birds darted in and out of the 18th century parish's eaves as they pulled scraps of earth they'd found to be useful in building their nests. Her head could not shake the image of her Tenna young and full of life. She imagined her having brunch with Freda. Lucy pictured her Tenna's blonde hair shiny and shimmering in the sun at a sidewalk café in midtown Manhattan. God did exist, somewhere. That's all Lucy would admit so far.

Back in her tiny apartment in Bronxville, Lucy prepared to go to work. The porcelain urn adorned her mantle. She put it there in January and its presence had become unobtrusive–like a cherished house guest. She suddenly noticed it and its appearance caused her to hyperventilate. She picked it up, as she often did, to get a sense of closure. It was cold and it emitted a coolness that she could feel by the warmth of other mantle pieces, and it tempted her to open it. It was a childish curiosity, like the first time a child steps up to an open-casket at a funeral and looks in only to satisfy it. Lucy's lips started to quiver for the first time since that night in January, and crying was on the tip of her tongue. She thought of all the lessons Tenna had taught her, the fun that they'd had and the lessons she continued to teach. Her muscles started to tremor and she felt weak and began to gag. She lunged forward and guided her convulsed body towards the urn and sent it crashing to the floor.

Lucy caught her breath and looked around her. She got a broom and started to clean up the broken vessel. She paused to savor the sound of its pieces cracking under her feet as she stepped. Her floors were hardwood and the jagged blue edges scratched the floor. The jar was empty and the thought fled through her mind that the urn had never contained ashes, that her aunt's death and return had been the subject of a dream. She picked a shard out of the dust pan and studied it closely, noticing how it twinkled in the light. She set the piece on the table and took out a magnifying glass. It felt like she was doing something wrong and blasphemous by examining it in the glass. The shard had a very thin film of a dusty residue.

Afterword

The stories "Ramifications for Schadenfreude" and "The Genuine Article" are fictional. However they are based on events in the author's own life. "Schadenfreude" follows Aaron Sullivan though a series of trials at college as he set out to unite with his biological mother. He questions his decision and his own Jewish faith. A host of characters, one of whom leads the Lutheran Campus Ministry, appear to Aaron as extracting joy from the anxiety each decision causes. "The Genuine Article" deals with the death of a loved one, a mother.

Finding me and Them: Stories of Assimilation is a family tree of sorts. It is my life, what happened to me as a kid, and how I chose to deal with it. I show whom I encountered, the bullies and the glad-handed sycophants. I write of my encounters with religious zealots, law men in Scotland and the junkies in downtown Minneapolis. I show my wanderings to find myself physically, emotionally, and spiritually. But the branches often connect as biological to adoptive families.

The book begins with me in my family, my only family for all intents and purposes. My gains are their gains, their losses are my losses. I experience all the normal growing pains, the adolescent rebellion and questioning if there's more in the world. I experience living in an urban area of Minneapolis after growing up in a middle-class suburb. I saw what I had that those urbanites did not; I saw what they had, opportunities, that I did not as a consequence of being disabled. But there is another family out there, a mother with a family (who I've met). I chose, in these stories, to fictionalize that family, or that idea of a woman that in different circumstances may have raised me. "Ramifications for Schadenfreude" tells the story relative to the nonfictional "A Lesson from the Shema." Aaron (me) questions the Jewish faith of the family that adopted him. He wonders if there is more to life, whether Christianity offers a sounder "insurance plan" if his meeting with his biological mother is disastrous. The fictional "Ramification for Schadenfreude" is related to the nonfiction "Power of Prayer." This story acts as a sequel to the fictional story. In "Power of Prayer" I learn, as a disabled adult with the conflicting precepts of my adoptive Jewish family, the power of Christian prayer and acceptance of Jesus, specifically as it applies to the disabled.

Families meet in reality. They meet in the spirit world. My biological mother passed away in 2012. That was the impetus for "The Genuine Article." In my adoptive family, my paternal grandmother passed on in 2003. That is the subject of the nonfictional "The Burial Plot." I explore the history, where previous members of my father's family were buried, and the logistical and Orthodox Jewish legal ramifications surrounding burial and an afterlife.

About the Author

*M*ichael Amram has been an indie author since 2005. He published his first novel, The Orthodoxy of Arrogance in 2013 and followed with Agent of Orange in 2014. Both novels present a distorted view of history, which Amram applies to his characters' lives. He is also an avid poet with three published collection. His individual poems and short works have been published in magazines. In 2011, he was accepted into the Minneapolis Loft Literary Center's mentor program. The manuscript for his first novel was chosen as a finalist. Amram lives with his wife in a suburb of Minneapolis. Visit him at his blog http://paulamram.blogspot.com

CPSIA information can be obtained
at www.ICGtesting.com
Printed in the USA
FSOW01n0103110517
34093FS